GENESIS 26-50
FROM START2FINISH

MICHAEL WHITWORTH

ISBN 978-1-941972-71-7

Published by Start2Finish
Branford, Florida 32008
start2finish.org

Printed in the United States of America

Cover Design: Evangela Creative

CONTENTS

1

THE FAITH OF ISAAC

GENESIS 25:19-26; 26

Objective: To appreciate God's faithfulness
to multiple generations of his people

INTRODUCTION

With the death of Abraham, the torch of faith passed to his unique son,
Isaac. Questions abound as we begin reading Isaac's story: Will he struggle
with his faith as did Abraham? Will he overcome as did his father? Will he
have Abraham's faith?

Though Isaac does not command center stage in Genesis for as long
as those who came before and after him, the stories about Isaac are intended by the narrator to illustrate the struggle—yet ultimately the maturity—
of his faith. Just as Abraham struggled with the promise of protection, so
did Isaac. But Isaac was also a dedicated servant of God and sought peace
when threatened by his enemies.

EXAMINATION

Read Genesis 25:19-28. With the phrase "These are the generations of,"
the narrator marks what is essentially a new chapter in the story of the

patriarchs. Abraham has been gathered to his people, and the covenant promises now have been passed fully to Isaac. Would he continue the rich legacy of faith? Well, we shall soon see since that faith was tested in the form of barrenness (it ran in the family).

Isaac responded to his wife's barrenness in a greater way than did his father. The text simply, yet beautifully, reads: "Isaac prayed to the LORD" (v. 21). Bill T. Arnold notes that "prayed" and "granted his prayer" in this verse are from the same Hebrew root, and thus proposes that "this turn-of-phrase denotes that Yahweh was emotively stirred into action, not against his will, but precisely to accomplish his will through the urging of his servant."

God indeed answered Isaac's prayer. "Rebekah his wife conceived." But this was a troubled pregnancy, for it says that her "children struggled together within her." Rebekah's discomfort was something more painful than "the baby kicking." When she couldn't take it anymore, she went to inquire of the Lord.

In response to her inquiry, God informed Rebekah that the struggle in her womb between her twin boys portended struggle between two nations, and in a reversal of the norm, "the older shall serve the younger" (v. 23). The whole lineage of Christ shows a preference for the younger over the older (Isaac vs. Ishmael, Judah vs. Reuben, Perez vs. Zerah, David vs. Eliab), which is another way of saying that God's election is based on his grace, not our merit (Rom. 11:6).

At birth, Esau "came out red," meaning he had a ruddy complexion; the same term is used to describe David (1 Sam. 16:12; 17:42). Esau was also born very hairy, which will become a significant detail later in the narrative. His twin brother came out grasping his heel, and the twin was named "Jacob." The name derived from the Hebrew noun meaning "heel." Figuratively, the word could also mean "deceive" (cf. 27:36; Jer. 9:4). No parent would name their kid "Liar," but this plot twist foreshadows events to come.

Read Genesis 26:1-5. When Abraham first arrived in Canaan, there had been a famine in the land forcing him to go to Egypt (12:10). This narrative is introduced with notice of another famine, and the narrator explicitly says it was not the same one Abraham had faced. Whether Abraham on that occasion had sought refuge in Egypt against God's will, we cannot be sure. But we know for a fact that God precluded Isaac from doing the same here. In the process, the Lord reaffirmed to Isaac the promises he had made to his father (cf. 12:1-3; 13:14-16; 22:17-18). If you gain a sense of déjà vu as you read the story, then it's not just you. This chapter gives us glimpses of Isaac's life that illustrate how he experienced blessings and frustrations similar to those of his father.

Read Genesis 26:6-16. Presumably at the Lord's direction (v. 2), "Isaac settled in Gerar" (v. 6) as his father once had (20:1). Just like his daddy had done, Isaac lied about his relationship with Rebekah out of fear for his own life. And like his father, Isaac was busted, though not in the same way. Notice there is a key difference in this story from the narratives of Gen. 12, 20; neither Abimelech, nor any other man in Gerar, ever touched Rebekah. Nonetheless, the king noticed Isaac sexually fondling his wife, instantly deduced their true relationship, and he became furious. Though the ESV reads in v. 8 that Isaac was "laughing with Rebekah," the translators admit in a note that the "Hebrew may suggest an intimate relationship," a fact reflected in other translations' use of "caressing."

As had been the case in Gen. 20, Abimelech was justifiably angry. He acknowledged that if someone had taken Rebekah as a wife, Isaac's deception "would have brought guilt upon us" (v. 10). And with that, Abimelech banned anyone from touching Isaac (violently) or Rebekah (sexually) under penalty of death.

It is certain that Isaac was to blame for the situation; his excuse was as flimsy as Abraham's had been. In Gen. 12, God had just promised Abraham that he would curse those who dishonored Abraham. Why did Abraham feel the need to lie to the Egyptians? In 15:1, Abraham received the assurance that God would shield him. In Gen. 19, God spared Lot from the destruction of Sodom for Abraham's sake. Why did Abraham feel the need to lie to the Philistines in Gen. 20? In 26:3-4, God affirmed the Abrahamic covenant to Isaac. Why did Isaac feel the need to lie to the Philistines?

Read Genesis 26:17-33. Despite Isaac's faithlessness, God was faithful (2 Tim. 2:13) to Isaac as he had been to his father. This is shown in the fact that, while in the area of Gerar, Isaac's harvest was 100x what he had planted. To get an idea of how ridiculously high this was, consider that the highest crop return recorded in ancient Near Eastern documents is 75x, and a yield of 2-3x was normal in medieval England. That Isaac's yield was this high is nothing short of remarkable, especially considering that it came in the middle of a famine!

The Lord kept blessing Isaac until he became wealthy just like his father. But as Abraham had discovered in Gen. 13, those blessings can sometimes cause problems. In Isaac's case, his blessings created significant envy among the Philistines, and he was expelled from the area. They also spitefully filled in the wells Isaac held rightful claim to since it had been his father's servants who had first dug them (presumably while Abraham had sojourned there in Gen. 20-21).

Isaac chose to leave peacefully instead of fight back, but he knew he was surrendering a valuable resource. He redug more of his father's wells and "gave them the names that his father had given them" (v. 18), which was a way of establishing clear ownership of a place—the prerogative to name something indicated authority and ownership. One of the wells was actually a freshwater spring, a very valuable find since a spring meant a continuous supply and would not dry up like a well could. But the Philistines ran Isaac off from that well, and then again from another; he named those wells "Esek" and "Sitnah," meaning "quarrel" and "accusation" respectively. Isaac finally found peace when he dug the third well, so he named it "Rehoboth," meaning "wide open spaces." But eventually, Isaac relocated to Beersheba. God appeared to him again and reaffirmed his promises and blessings. Isaac responded in the way his father often had: he built an altar (cf. 12:8; 13:18).

It was also at Beersheba that Isaac was visited by Abimelech, who had in tow his counselor Ahuzzath and military commander Phicol. Abimelech wanted to secure a treaty with Isaac. He acknowledged that God was the source of Isaac's wealth, though he seems oblivious to the mistreatment Isaac had suffered at the hands of his countrymen (v. 29; cf. 21:26). When they first arrived, Isaac appeared indignant. But he evidently settled down and confirmed the treaty by inviting them to a feast. The scene ends with Isaac's servants informing him that they had successfully dug another well; God's blessings were indeed great in the life of Abraham's son.

APPLICATION

The Struggle to Believe. There is no good reason for Abraham and Isaac to have acted as they did, lying about their relationships with their wives. But their behavior is a reminder that we all are weak at times in living out the promises of God. Our failures do not mean God is less trustworthy, but that we need to do a better job of living as if his promises are *real* and *reliable*, because they are on both counts. Abraham and Isaac both discovered that it is one thing to stand in awe as God reaffirms to you the blessing of the ages; it is quite another thing altogether to live in light of that blessing in the cruel, hard world of reality. God's people have always been called to "walk by faith, not by sight" (2 Cor. 5:7).

Blessed Are Peacemakers. A wise man once told me, "People want you to succeed, but not too much." God's people will experience conflict with those envious of our success and blessing. We would do well to follow Isaac's example and "move on" from such people. Allow them to wallow in their envy and insecurity. It may not help you to confront it—if a person covets your blessing, then you're likely the last one they want giving them a spiritual wake-up call. By moving on from springs of conflict and wells of accusation, you show yourself to be a peacemaker. Who knows? Maybe others will envy your agreeable spirit! It takes faith to abandon blessings, confident that God can restore what we have lost. But if we truly believe that God is greater than any adversary we might ever face, this is the course we will choose. Remember, our God is peace, and he calls us to pursue the same (2 Cor. 13:11; 2 Tim. 2:22).

The Faithfulness of God. That God took the time to reaffirm his covenant to Isaac (and later to Jacob) should give us pause. If we are not careful, we can become plagued by a generational arrogance that leads us to believe we are the linchpin of the church, and once the "next generation" comes along, things will be ruined. But God is more faithful to his people than that, and he always has been. The same God who affirmed his covenant to multiple generations of the patriarchs is the same God who promised, through Christ, that the gates of hell would never prevail against his church, and that we are more than conquerors through the Lord Jesus Christ. The next time you are filled with dread over what the next generation may face, remind yourself that God is always faithful to his people throughout multiple generations and across the centuries.

CONCLUSION

Just as quickly as he came to dominate the biblical stage, Isaac becomes a supporting actor once again. He will recede into the background as his sons, Jacob and Esau, become the main players in Genesis' drama. But his legacy of faith and peace endures even today. "Father, help us trust in your promises and make peace with our enemies as Isaac taught us to do."

QUESTIONS FOR REFLECTION

1. What details of Gen. 26 point back to the life of Abraham? Why did the narrator record similar stories concerning father and son?

2. Why is it significant that God reaffirmed the covenant of Abraham to Isaac?

3. How did Abimelech learn the truth about Isaac and Rebekah's relationship?

4. In the midst of a famine, what was the yield of Isaac's harvest? Why is this significant?

5. What was Isaac's response whenever he was run off from one of his wells?

QUESTIONS FOR DISCUSSION

1. Have you struggled to believe that God's promises are both real and reliable? How so?

2. Discuss this statement: "It is one thing to stand in awe as God reaffirms to you the blessing of the ages; it is quite another thing altogether to live in light of that blessing in the cruel, hard world of reality."

3. When others become jealous of your success, what is the best response?

4. Have you ever been forced to abandon a blessing in order to keep the peace? What was that experience like?

5. Have you witnessed God's faithfulness to your parents or children/grandchildren? How so?

2

JACOB & ESAU, PT. 1

GENESIS 25:27-34; 27

Objective: To discover how God furthers his purposes
through dysfunction and disobedience

INTRODUCTION

Though Cain killed Abel out of jealousy, Jacob and Esau win the biblical
award for sibling rivalry. In the rest of Scripture, they become the epitome
of fraternal strife—"I have loved Jacob but Esau I have hated," God once
declared (Mal. 1:2-3).

In this lesson, we discover the origin of their feud. God used unhealthy
parental favoritism and fraternal strife to advance his plan for Abraham's
seed. Though Rebekah and Jacob acted deceitfully in Gen. 27, they also
acted consistent with God's will for the two brothers. In this way, Jacob
and Esau stand not just for sibling rivalry, but as a testament to a God who
works his perfect plan in spite of all the dysfunction of our lives.

EXAMINATION

Read Genesis 25:27-34. Though born as twins, Jacob and Esau were polar opposites as adults. Esau was an outdoorsman and kind of redneck-ish,

while Jacob was said to be a "quiet man," probably meaning "well-cultured" or "civilized." But their unique personalities made them the favorite of different parents.

This story opens with a perfect anecdote for the twins' polar personalities: Jacob cooking and Esau hunting. In actuality, Esau came in "exhausted" from a hunt; he noticed his brother preparing a delicious soup and demanded some. Jacob seized the opportunity to lay claim to his brother's birthright; he would give food to his starving brother in exchange for it. Esau didn't blink at the offer, but Jacob demanded he swear to it. The rest of the narrative is hurriedly wrapped up: Esau "ate and drank and rose and went his way" (v. 34).

But the narrator cannot turn away from the narrative before offering a final criticism: "Thus Esau despised his birthright." Considering the things that Moses never explicitly censures in the Genesis text (drunkenness, lying, incest), this is a serious statement. The birthright due the firstborn son was a precious thing. According to Deut. 21:17, the firstborn was entitled to two portions of the estate. For example, if there were six sons in the family, the inheritance was divided seven ways, and the oldest received two portions; if there were three sons, the oldest received half the estate (i.e. two-fourths).

In this particular case, Esau could expect to receive a minimum two-thirds of the inheritance. And when Esau so carelessly gave his birthright away, the original audience would have recoiled in horror at someone being so careless with something so precious. Even in the secular literature and legal codes of the ancient Near East, this was completely unheard of.

Read Genesis 27. In ancient times, it was customary for the family patriarch to give a blessing to his children before death. This was always considered to be an important event carrying significant ramifications for the future. By this point, Isaac was about 137 years old. While he wasn't on his deathbed (chronologically, he didn't die until a year before Joseph's ascendency in Egypt), he still wanted to put his affairs in order "just in case." He was also going blind, so he summoned Esau and asked him to prepare a special meal, at which point he planned to give Esau the blessing due the firstborn.

Rebekah overheard Isaac's command to Esau. Because she favored Jacob, she initiated a plan to deceive her blind husband, something the Law of Moses would have denounced (Lev. 19:14; Deut. 27:18). There is absolutely nothing favorable we can say about the actions of Rebekah and Jacob except that they were used by God to further his divine purposes. There is no denying that, as John Calvin put it, Jacob's "seeking the blessing by fraud, and insinuating himself into the possession of it by falsehood, was contrary to faith." And he was clearly less concerned with the morality of his actions than he was what would happen to him if he were caught (cf. v. 12).

But Rebekah seems worthy of greater blame since she played the greater role. This ruse was no mere suggestion on her part, but rather a "command" to Jacob (v. 8). By preparing the food Isaac liked, dressing Jacob up in Esau's clothes, and placing animal skins on Jacob to make him feel as hairy as his brother, Rebekah sought for Jacob the position of leadership in the clan. She may have been acting consistent with the oracle she had received at birth, but she should have realized that God does not need the immoral aid of his children to accomplish his purposes in the world.

The sudden return of "Esau" did not seem right to Isaac. The voice had to be Jacob's, but his other senses (the feel of Esau's hairy arms, the strong odor of his scent) led Isaac to conclude that Esau indeed stood before him, so he commenced with the blessing.

Note the timing of the next scene: "As soon as…" (v. 30). It would be easy to assume that timing throughout the patriarchal narratives (e.g. 24:15; 37:25) is merely coincidental. But Genesis adamantly maintains that God directs the events as they unfold. No sooner had Jacob exited than Esau entered with precisely the meal his father had requested. Isaac was horrified when he realized what had happened. It may confuse us as to why he couldn't simply annul the blessing; deception had to be legitimate grounds for doing so. But in the ancient Near East, the spoken word was not simply recalled by honorable individuals; they knew it was like putting toothpaste back into the tube. How much more so a blessing which, once spoken, had a life and power all its own and could not be undone (cf. Num. 30:2; Judg. 11:30-35)?

Meanwhile, Esau was livid. His outburst, "Is he not rightly named Jacob? For he has cheated me these two times" (v. 36), is a deliberate pun since the Hebrew words for "Jacob" and "cheated" are from the same root. What is most alarming is that Esau fully intended to kill his brother, making him almost as bad as Cain.

It is painful when a valuable object, once the recipient of our carelessness or scorn, is taken away from us. But while he had scorned his birthright, we are never told whether Esau had scorned his blessing; these were two different things. Nonetheless, Isaac had no other blessing to give than one that resigned Esau to an inferior future. Isaac's prophecy regarding Esau serving, then breaking his brother's yoke, was fulfilled centuries later when David subjugated the Edomites (2 Sam. 8:14).

APPLICATION

God's Immutable Will. One of the hallmarks of Genesis is the power of God to use human sin for his own purposes. Through Jacob's many acts of deceit in his life, God worked to bring Judah into the world; through Judah, God gave us the strength of David, the wisdom of Solomon, and the atonement of Christ. To paraphrase Alexander Maclaren, the wicked deeds of evil men cannot sidetrack the stream of divine purpose anymore than a child can divert the Mississippi River with a mud dam. The greatest example of this magnificent truth is Judas' betrayal of our Lord. Such an evil deed was necessary for the salvation of our souls (cf. 1 Cor. 2:8). Bill T. Arnold puts it this way: "God's purposes are not thwarted by human sin, but rather advanced by it through his good graces." This did not exempt Judas from eternal condemnation (Matt. 26:24), but Christians should stand in awestruck wonder at God's ability to take something so terrible and remake it into something so wonderful (Rom. 11:33).

Esau's Legacy. It is admittedly obscure in the ESV, but Esau requested of Jacob "a *swallow* of that red stuff there" (25:30 NASU). This unique choice of words portrays an awkward Esau wanting just a little bit of stew in order to gratify a base instinct, no matter the cost. The New Testament uses Esau as a cautionary tale for the sexually immoral. "See to it … that no one is sexually immoral or unholy like Esau, who sold his birthright for a single meal" (Heb. 12:15-16). The Jewish rabbis alleged that Esau was promiscuous with married women, and in light of this passage from Hebrews, there may be some truth to that. Either way, Esau embodies the person who cannot resist temptation in exchange for some future reward, but would rather take a little here-and-now, even if it means surrendering something greater in the hereafter. Sexual temptation specifically appeals to the hunger of the flesh, persuading us to forget about the glory and honor of an undefiled marriage bed (Heb. 13:4). But as was the case for Esau, the tradeoff is never worth it, and only leads to many years (if not a lifetime) of heartache.

CONCLUSION

The end of Gen. 27 leaves us with a fuming Esau, a fearful Rebekah, a despondent Isaac, and a soon-to-be exiled Jacob. For anyone with a broken family history, the painful bitterness of this scene is palpable. But God was not through with Abraham's seed. He would continue to advance his purposes. As Jacob packed his bags and fled from everything he had ever known, he had to have felt as if his life was over in one sense. Little did he know that God's work in his life was just beginning.

QUESTIONS FOR REFLECTION

1. Though born as twins, in what ways were Jacob and Esau polar opposites?

2. What exactly was the firstborn birthright in Old Testament times?

3. Would the Law of Moses have denounced Rebekah and Jacob's actions in Gen. 27? If so, why?

4. Why couldn't Isaac simply renounce his blessing on Jacob on the grounds of deception and pronounce a new one on Esau?

5. In his anger, what pun did Esau make concerning Jacob's name?

6. Have you been the victim of parental favoritism or sibling rivalry? How so? Did any good come from it? If so, how?

QUESTIONS FOR DISCUSSION

1. The narrator says that Esau "despised" his birthright (Gen. 25:34). What does this mean and why is this a significant statement?

2. Was the timing of Esau's return in Gen. 27 coincidental or providential? Explain your answer.

3. Discuss this statement: "God's purposes are not thwarted by human sin, but rather advanced by it through his good graces."

4. Have you witnessed God's goodness in spite of dysfunction or disobedience? How so?

5. How and why does Esau serve as a cautionary tale for the sexually immoral?

3

JACOB AT BETHEL

GENESIS 28

Objective: To discover how God reaffirmed
to Jacob the covenant of Abraham

INTRODUCTION

With Esau's anger boiling against him, Jacob fled his family home to live
with his uncle, Laban. So far in the story, Jacob does not appear to be too
spiritual, nor is he interested in serving the God of his fathers. But in a
tremendous act of grace, God appeared to Jacob at Bethel and reaffirmed
the promises and covenant he had first extended to Abraham. The story reminds us that God mercifully meets us where we are, instead of demanding
that we mature and rise to his level before becoming his servants.

EXAMINATION

Read Genesis 28:1-9. After Jacob's deception had landed him the firstborn's blessing, Rebekah became alarmed at Esau's intention to kill Jacob.
She did not want to lose one son to murder and the other to exile or retribution all in the same day. To avoid losing both sons, Rebekah sent Jacob
to live with her brother until Esau simmered down.

Instead of coming and expressing her fear that Esau would murder Jacob, Rebekah shrewdly couched her request to Isaac in terms of her disgust for Esau's wives, a feeling she knew her husband shared. Sure enough, Jacob was summoned to his father's side and given a strict command not to marry a local woman, but to head to the home of Laban and marry one of his daughters. Isaac called on El Shaddai to bless Jacob and expressed the hope that his son would inherit the covenant promises of Abraham (vv. 3-4).

Finally, we are left with a parting image of a very dense-headed Esau. At the very end of Gen. 26, we are told that Esau married two Canaanite women named Judith and Basemath, thereby departing from the wishes of his grandfather and the example of his father. Esau's choice of wives greatly embittered Isaac and Rebekah, so why he remained his father's favorite is anyone's guess. As James McKeown puts it, Esau is throughout these narratives "portrayed as someone who tries hard but who does not really understand the main issues." Even now, Esau recognized his parents were upset with his marrying Canaanite women, but in a last ditch effort to please his parents, he married Ishmael's daughter Mahalath. A third wife does not make a right.

Read Genesis 28:10-22. Jacob was now on the run from his brother's fierce fury; his perilous journey would be over 500 miles, and it would have taken at least two or three days to cover the almost sixty miles between Beersheba and Bethel. But a few days into his journey of escape, God appeared to Jacob in a mighty way in order to ease his anxiety. It was a noteworthy occasion since this was the first time God spoke directly to Jacob, the third generation of the Abrahamic covenant.

According to the mythology of the ancient Near East, it was often thought that if one slept in a sacred place (e.g. a temple or high place), the gods would reveal a revelation. But the narrator completely disassociates that pagan concept from this event in Jacob's life. The overnight stop was unplanned and circumstantial, the place (until the end of the story) was unknown, and it was God who took the initiative in speaking to Jacob. We cannot choose the times that God powerfully makes himself known in our lives; if we could, such moments wouldn't be acts of grace.

While sleeping, Jacob envisioned "a stairway" (v. 12 NIV; cf. ESV note) rising to heaven with angels going up and down, not as if on parade, but going out and returning from missions on behalf of God. From his position atop the stairway, God presided over the process. The Lord was thus revealing that these "ministering spirits" would be working as his agents on

Jacob's behalf (Heb. 1:14; cf. Psa. 91:11; Zech. 1:10).

In the dream, God affirmed to him that the covenant promises made to Abraham and Isaac would also perpetuate to Jacob. Specifically, he would inherit the Promised Land, his posterity would be very numerous, and he would be an agency of blessing to the nations (vv. 13-14). But more relevant to Jacob's immediate dilemma was the next promise: "Behold, I am with you and will keep you wherever you go, and will bring you back to this land. For I will not leave you until I have done what I have promised you" (v. 15). Jacob may have been able to swindle Esau and deceive Isaac, but the Lord held sovereign sway over Jacob's future. "The Deceiver" didn't have to deceive to gain a bright future for himself.

I'm sure the covenant promises of land, children, and blessing mattered to Jacob, but I think the thought of never seeing his home and parents again mattered to him a great deal more on this occasion. So God spoke to those anxious worries. Jacob was assured that God's presence—his sovereign guidance and protection—would not end until Jacob returned home. And it didn't matter where Jacob journeyed; God's efficacy was not limited to Canaan.

As had been the case with Abraham and Isaac, God's promises meant God's provision, and this is a key realization; Jacob struggled mightily to trust in God's provision in a greater way than his fathers ever did. It proved profoundly difficult for Jacob to eschew the lifestyle his name embodied. He was a deceiver by nature, one who sought to get ahead at others' expense. This directly contradicted the life of faith God was proposing to him. Jacob could choose to trick or trust, but real blessings come only through faith.

Jacob's fear and amazement the following morning is understandable; how could God exhibit so much favor toward one so undeserving? At this stage in the narrative, Jacob has been no saint. He has certainly done nothing to merit the blessings and promises God had extended to him. But neither have I, nor you, done anything to merit God's favor. He extends to us the greatest blessing of all: salvation through his Son, that we might enjoy every spiritual blessing (Eph. 1:3). Such an offer is made on the basis of his grace, not our goodness, and we accept it through whole-hearted faith and obedience to his gospel (Eph. 2:8-10; Rom. 6:17).

Consistent with the idea that name-change marked important events, Jacob gave a new name to the place where he had spent the previous night. No longer would it be known as Luz, but Bethel, meaning "God's house." Jacob made a vow to God: if he was indeed given divine protection and provision, Jacob would return to Bethel and give to God a tenth of his possessions.

APPLICATION

God's Gracious Revelation. God no longer reveals himself as conspicuously as he did in this passage. It is not because God is somehow impotent, but because his final word was spoken through Jesus Christ, his Son (Heb. 1:1-2). That said, there are moments when God makes his presence in our lives known in a powerful way. Whether through the words of a timely hymn or in the warm embrace of a friend, God suffocates us with his presence when we most need it. If you stop to think, there are no doubt moments in your past when God made himself known powerfully. As he did for Jacob, divine promises were reaffirmed for you in those moments, including arguably his most precious promise of all—"I am with you always, to the end of the age" (Matt. 28:20).

Jacob's Vow. Did Jacob have any business making his vow to God at the end of the chapter? One the one hand, he's declaring his dependence on God. But on closer examination, one wonders if this isn't Jacob wheeling and dealing once again. In the Old Testament, vows were often made under duress, and thus Israel was warned against making a rash vow and not keeping it. Much better than wheeling and dealing with God in times of duress is to respond simply in faith to whatever circumstances face us, confident that God will either deliver us or use our suffering for his glory.

Jesus & Jacob's Ladder. In the Gospel of John, Jesus echoed this narrative when he said to his disciples, "Truly, truly, I say to you, you will see heaven opened, and the angels of God ascending and descending on the Son of Man" (1:51). What did Jesus mean? By virtue of the Crucifixion and Resurrection, Christ is the mediator between God and man (1 Tim. 2:5). He himself is God's greatest blessing and promise. Just as God reveled himself to Jacob at Bethel with a ladder of angels ascending and descending, he reveals himself to us in the person and work of Christ. How grateful we should be that God saw fit to affirm himself and his promises through One who will never leave nor forsake us (2 Tim. 2:13).

CONCLUSION

Jacob's experience at Bethel reminds me of the experiences I often observed at church camps I attended as a teenager. These weeks in the summer were always special, lending a devout camper a "mountain-top" spiritual experience—an emotional high. These camp sessions provided a "bubble" or retreat atmosphere where we could reconnect with God and rededicate our lives to him. But when we returned home, we also reentered the harsh world of reality. It's one thing to dedicate yourself to God; it's another to live it. This would prove to be Jacob's struggle—his spirit may very well have been willing, but his flesh remained quite weak.

QUESTIONS FOR REFLECTION

1. What did Esau do in an attempt to smooth things over with his parents? Why was this a bad idea?

2. What did Jacob's "ladder" or staircase symbolize?

3. What was the most relevant portion of God's promise to Jacob?

4. What name did Jacob give to the place where he experienced this dream? What does the name mean?

5. vow did Jacob make as he departed from Bethel?

QUESTIONS FOR DISCUSSION

1. Describe your perspective of Esau's place in his family? In your opinion, did he feel as if he "belonged"? Why/why not?

2. Was God's appearance to Jacob in a dream an act of grace? If so, how?

3. In what ways has God powerfully reaffirmed his presence and provision in your life?

4. What other significant biblical events happened at Bethel?

5. Discuss this statement: "God's promises mean God's provision."

4

JACOB & LABAN

GENESIS 29-31

Objective: To observe the sin in Jacob's/Laban's
treatment of others and the family dysfunction it fostered

INTRODUCTION

I'm sort of a fan of reality TV that features contests. One of my favorites
is the Food Network's *Cutthroat Kitchen*, the show where talented chefs
prepare various dishes while sabotaging their competition. In comparison
to other reality shows, such as *The Bachelor* or *The Bachelorette*, *Cutthroat
Kitchen* is quite tame.

But regardless of how "tame" they might seem, all of reality TV reveals
our tendency as fallen sinners to dehumanize others in order to get ahead.
This is the problem presented by Jacob, Laban, Leah, and Rachel in this story. In one way or another, they all dehumanized one another—they failed
to treat one another as souls created in God's image—and dysfunction began to reign. Their story is also a reminder that dysfunction can take root
in families as a vicious cycle, and only God's sovereign grace can break the
cycle once and for all.

EXAMINATION

Read Genesis 29:1-30. In spite of their similarities, one cannot help but notice a stark difference between Jacob's arrival in Haran and the arrival of Abraham's servant in Gen. 24. Both stories involved a well, but Abraham's caravan had been loaded with riches; Jacob came empty-handed. Abraham's servant committed his mission to prayer, but if Jacob prayed, we don't know about it. He seems to have stumbled onto the scene resolved to survive on his self-sufficiency. His ability to remove the stone by himself does not spark awareness of God's presence.

And when he discovered he had arrived at his intended destination, he did not thank God profusely as Abraham's servant had done. Rather, he became instantly infatuated with Rachel, his uncle Laban's younger daughter. One might say he experienced love at first sight with Rachel. Leah was pretty, but the text presents Rachel as stunningly beautiful. Notice that, as soon as Jacob saw Rachel for the first time, he flexed his muscles for her, after which he "kissed Rachel and wept aloud" (v. 11).

After he had stayed a month, Jacob was offered wages for his labor to Laban. Why should Jacob work for free? Since he was so smitten with Rachel, Jacob asked for her hand in marriage in exchange for work. He agreed to work seven years in order to pay the bride price, and this was not an unusual arrangement in the ancient Near East. This payment was a sort of insurance in the event of divorce, desertion, or death. An average bride price would have been thirty or forty shekels. Since the average annual wage of a laborer was ten shekels, Jacob was being forced to pay almost double the customary amount for Rachel.

When the time came for the wedding, Laban threw the customary celebration. The text does not say so explicitly, hence we cannot know for sure, but it is suspected that Jacob was quite intoxicated due to the party. The Hebrew word for "feast" involved drunkenness (cf. 1 Sam. 25:36; Esth. 1:3, 7-8; Isa. 25:6; Jer. 51:39), so that may be why Jacob did not recognize which sister he spent the night with. The narrator invites us to be as shocked as Jacob was (v. 25). The Deceiver had been deceived!

Laban's excuse was that it was not their custom to allow a younger sister to marry out-of-turn, but why hadn't he explained this before? Jacob was clearly not happy, and though he was permitted to marry Rachel also (he first had to finish the marriage week with Leah), he would have to work another seven years to pay his debt.

Finally, what is so unfortunate in this story is how Leah, through no fault of her own, was caught in the crossfire of a contentious relationship between Jacob and Laban. As we are about to see, the names of her children bore witness to her very troubled marriage.

Read Genesis 29:31-30:24. A regular theme of Genesis appears yet again: the barrenness of Israel's matriarchs. God is the sovereign giver of life, and it is his prerogative to open or close a womb. In this case, he gave Leah the blessing of children because of the heartache she felt in her marriage; Rachel, on the other hand, remained barren for quite a while.

We are also told that Jacob "hated" Leah, but a better understanding here is "loved less" or "unloved" (cf. Deut. 21:15; Mal. 1:3; Matt. 6:24). Leah believed her bearing children would give Jacob a reason to love her more, but she proved sadly mistaken. These two sisters are at tragic odds with one another in this narrative since both have what the other does not. Leah's fertility, which is attributed directly to God's blessing, became an object of jealousy between Leah and Rachel. In response to her own barrenness, Rachel blamed God as Sarah had done (16:2). She suggested Jacob take her servant as a surrogate wife; children born to that relationship would legally be Rachel's. If God refused to give her a child, she would take the matter into her own hands.

Sure enough, two more kids were born to Jacob through Bilhah. In spite of her four sons, Leah became intensely jealous of Rachel's maidservant, and she gave her own to Jacob. And just when you thought this family feud couldn't get any worse, Leah's oldest son brought her a prize from the fields "in the days of wheat harvest" (i.e. about May). The aroma of mandrake roots, sometimes called "love apples," was considered an aphrodisiac in ancient times (cf. Song of Sol. 7:13) and a cure for sterility.

Rachel likely thought that, with these mandrakes, she would not only become fertile, but also irresistible to her husband. He would then stop sleeping with Leah altogether, and Leah would become increasingly irrelevant. Rachel in effect said, "Fine, sleep with Jacob tonight. It will be the last time you do so if I can help it." But in divine irony, Leah conceived Issachar on that very night, his name acting as a memorial of the night Leah had "hired" Jacob to sleep with her. And God wasn't through blessing Leah—she gave birth to a sixth(!) son, Zebulun, and a daughter, Dinah.

Finally, "God remembered Rachel" just as he had remembered Noah

(8:1). In other words, the Lord turned his attention to delivering Rachel from her suffering and opened her womb. God succeeded where Rachel's manipulation and mandrakes had failed.

Read Genesis 30:25-43. All the while, the relationship between Laban and Jacob deteriorated rapidly. Laban had mistreated him in more ways than tricking him into marrying his two daughters. Weary of the injustice, Jacob had wanted to return home, but what had kept him around was the barrenness of his favorite wife. So it was not until Rachel had given birth to Joseph that Jacob expressed his desire to be released from service. Laban, however, had "learned by divination" that he had been blessed by God because of Jacob (v. 27). Why should Laban lose an employee he knew to be so valuable?

For the first time since arriving at Laban's house, Jacob was in a superior bargaining position. He devised a scheme whereby he would increase his flocks. He would be allowed to keep every newborn sheep or goat that was speckled, spotted, or dark-colored. Such animals usually made up only a small part of the herd, less than 20% (most sheep were white, and goats were dark), and the average commission for a shepherd would have been more than this. Laban thought he was getting the better deal, but in his greed, he went so far as to remove all of the current speckled, spotted, or dark-colored animals from his herds to keep Jacob from gaining a "starter herd" of such animals. Jacob had the last laugh, however. Not only did this not deter his ability to grow a large herd, but the three-day distance gave him a head-start when he escaped from Laban six years later.

Jacob took branches and peeled part of the bark away so that the branches looked to be striped, i.e. alternating bark/no bark. He seemed to have believed, quite superstitiously (and incorrectly), that if the animals looked at these alternating colors while mating, their offspring would be multi-colored, and would thus belong to Jacob and not Laban. He also made sure the stronger animals mated with one another in order to produce a superior flock for himself, a process that makes sense to modern readers since we understand the principles of genetics and heredity.

There are some elements in this section that are admittedly confusing, but the text makes two things very clear. Jacob became a very wealthy man as is evident from the flocks, servants, and other animals he acquired. But the text is also unequivocal that God was the real source of Jacob's prosperity. Whether Jacob actually believed in the superstitions, or simply employed them to fool Laban, the take-away here is that God is the sole arbiter of life and blessing, a point on which Genesis is definitive.

Read Genesis 31. After twenty years of working for Laban, Jacob had had enough. The straw that broke the camel's back was the Lord speaking to him directly (v. 3). With that, Jacob called a family meeting. In his speech to his wives, we learn the depths of Laban's mistreatment (vv. 14-15). The bride price for each of his daughters had been seven years of labor, and Laban should have stored away seven years of wages for both Leah and Rachel as insurance policies in case of death, divorce, or desertion. But he had apparently burned through the money already, so they were just fine with leaving their selfish father behind.

Jacob and his family escaped while Laban was out shearing sheep, but Laban quickly caught up with them. He was understandably angry, but God had warned him about retribution (v. 24). When Jacob and his family had fled, Rachel had stolen her father's household gods (v. 19), and Laban thought Jacob was the culprit. Whatever Rachel's reason for taking them, her father clearly cherished these idols. When Laban attempted to search her tent, she used menstruation as an excuse for "not getting up" (we have no idea if she was lying). Whether Rachel meant to insinuate such, the narrator certainly intends for us to see this as a contemptible rejection of these idols having any real power (cf. Lev. 15:20).

When Laban returned from his search empty-handed, Jacob released an absolute torrent of verbal rage on his head. Using language very similar to that of a lawsuit, Jacob vented his frustration at the mistreatment he had suffered while working for Laban. It was humiliating enough that Laban had accused him of stealing personal property, but Jacob was also angry that Laban had been quite the unpleasant employer.

But embedded within Jacob's tirade is the belief that God had mitigated his suffering (v. 42). It had been God who had allowed him to prosper under such difficult circumstances. It had been God who had rebuked Laban. This is only consistent with the promise God had made to Abraham—the promise to curse those who dared dishonor the patriarch (12:3). And while the New Testament forbids us to seek revenge against those who mistreat us, especially those in power, we are also promised that those who dare to harm God's anointed will find themselves under his curse forever (2 Thess. 1:6-9).

Laban was clearly not happy with Jacob's rebuke, but he also realized he could not compel Jacob to do as he wished. God had spoken. So Laban offered a treaty. Before our eyes is the establishment of the house of Laban and the house of Jacob as two separate entities. The pile of stones had the force of a political boundary that must not be crossed. Most notably, Laban invoked "the God of Nahor" in a way that makes clear he considered such a deity to be different from the one patronized by Abraham's family. Henceforth, Jacob and Laban would be two "distinct peoples." Laban would remain polytheistic, but Jacob would go on to a deeper relationship with his God, known here as the "Fear of his father Isaac" (v. 53).

APPLICATION

Reap What You Sow. For much of his life, Jacob was a pathological liar and deceiver. But Laban gave him a dose of his own medicine by giving him Leah in marriage when Jacob believed he was getting Rachel. In such situations, we are tempted to exclaim, "What goes around, comes around." The Bible expresses the same reality in a different way; the apostle Paul warned, "Do not be deceived: God is not mocked, for whatever one sows, that will he also reap" (Gal. 6:7). None of us are perfect. We have all mistreated others and consequently reap what we had sown. But Christians are always to be interested in redemption, so we must transform those painful moments into appreciation for the suffering we have caused with our own sin.

Dehumanization. There was an atrocious tendency toward dehumanization in Laban's family. Laban believed he had a higher obligation to tradition than to his nephew, so he deceived Jacob by giving him Leah, not Rachel. Laban was intent on milking Jacob for every economic advantage he could, and he evidently was so greedy that he stole from his daughters a portion of money rightfully theirs. No less guilty is Rachel; in the mandrake scene, the horror of what actually transpires should not be lost on us—she pimps out her husband to his first wife! Broken relationships of any kind are most always the product of one person dehumanizing another, of a failure to regard others as precious souls made in God's image and in need of God's love. No wonder, then, that Jesus considered there to be two great commands of equal significance, not just one: love God and love others (Matt. 22:36-39). Indeed, all of God's rules for human relationships spring from this simple command: "Love" (cf. Rom. 13:8-10).

Faith on the Job. Though work-place abuse is nowhere near as epidemic as it once was, it is still possible to serve an unreasonable employer. What is a biblical response to mistreatment by those in power over us? Jacob certainly suffered under Laban's unfair employment demands, but he learned to deal with such mistreatment from a position of faith, not fear. Faith demands that we serve our bosses/masters as we would Christ—"not by the way of eye-service, as people-pleasers, but as bondservants of Christ, doing the will of God from the heart" (Eph. 6:5-6). After he had said almost identical things to the Colossians, the apostle Paul added that any employer who dares mistreat us will be punished severely by a God who does not show partiality or favoritism (Col. 3:25; cf. Eph. 6:9). In the end, Christians suffering mistreatment from an unreasonable master must remember that those things most precious to us cannot be affected by anyone in anyway (Matt. 10:28), and that "from the Lord you will receive the inheritance as your reward. You are serving the Lord Christ" (Col. 3:24).

CONCLUSION

In many ways, the nation of Israel experienced for themselves what Jacob endured at Laban's hands. In Exodus, Pharaoh had manipulated and cheated Israel for a long time; it would have been easy to think that God was no match for Pharaoh's craftiness. But the suffering of God's people is not evidence of God's impotence. When it seems as if his will is being put at a disadvantage, it takes great faith to believe otherwise. It requires great faith in things not seen. "Setback" is not a part of God's vocabulary, for God always moves forward. In spite of all the sin and dysfunction we manage to concoct (and sometimes through it!), God is faithful in achieving his purposes in the world.

QUESTIONS FOR REFLECTION

1. Why did Laban deceive Jacob in giving him Leah, not Rachel?

2. Why did Jacob not realize whom he was marrying?

3. What did the names of Leah's and Rachel's sons (as well as the sons of their maidservants) represent?

4. Though he practiced a few ancient agricultural superstitions in order to grow his herd, who was really responsible for Jacob's success as a breeder?

5. When he caught up to Jacob and his family, what prevented Laban from harming them in his anger?

6. Whom did Jacob credit with mitigating his suffering under Laban's heavy hand?

QUESTIONS FOR DISCUSSION

1. Jacob's and Laban's penchant to dehumanize others as a means to an end fostered a culture of dysfunction, which was perpetuated to the next generation (Leah and Rachel, Joseph and his brothers). In your experience, how have you seen dehumanization cultivate dysfunction?

2. In his warning to Laban, God effectively established a circle of protection around Jacob. Why did God do this? Did Jacob deserve this divine protection? Explain.

3. How has God made you reap in the present what you have sown in your sinful past? Though often painful, how is this evidence of God's grace?

4. How does Jacob's example in these chapters encourage us to endure the injustice or severity of an ungodly employer?

5. What hope do Christians have when they endure suffering and mistreatment at the hands of others?

5

JACOB & ESAU, PT. 2

GENESIS 32-33

Objective: To reflect on Jacob's
reconciliation with both Esau and God

INTRODUCTION

This section of Genesis marks a new era in Jacob's life. He had made a covenant of peace with Laban and continued his return to Canaan. However, his homecoming remained marred by nightmares of his petty dealings with Esau. It had been twenty years, but had Esau's rage softened? Had it festered and intensified like a nasty sore? Jacob had no way of knowing as he and his family journeyed towards the Promised Land. And we readers have our own questions. Is Jacob a changed man after his midnight struggle? Will he continue to be duplicitous? Will he be more trusting? Though Jacob's reconciliation with Esau is the dominant story line, it is Jacob's reconciliation with God that is the real story.

EXAMINATION

Read Genesis 32:1-11. After his encounter with Laban, Jacob continued home accompanied by angels. The appearance of these heavenly beings had marked his departure years before (28:10-12), and they now signaled his return. Jacob named the camp Mahanaim ("two camps"), an acknowledgment that both he and God had been encamped there. The Hebrew phrase translated "God's camp" elsewhere signifies a large army (1 Chron. 12:22). To a casual observer, Jacob had been fending for himself since fleeing from his brother so many years earlier, but he had in actuality been under God's sovereign watch the entire time despite his repeated failures.

Encouraged by God's presence, Jacob sent messengers to Esau to give advance notice of his arrival, rather than risk the appearance of sneaking around his brother's back. Jacob knew it was time to face the music. Jacob intimated he was completely willing to buy Esau off if necessary. The messengers returned to Jacob with news that Esau was on his way with 400 men. Elsewhere in the Old Testament, this number is often used of a militia (cf. 1 Sam. 22:2; 25:13; 30:10), so it's no wonder that Jacob was terrified when he heard the news. He couldn't very well return the way he had come; life under Laban's thumb was no life at all. So Jacob put a plan into action intended to minimize his losses should Esau attack.

But notice that the patriarch also threw himself upon God's mercy and prayed for protection (vv. 9-12). Jacob's self-sufficiency was running out. If God's protection was not sought, he had no chance against Esau's wrath. Jacob was learning to trust in the God of his fathers, but it is significant that nowhere in this prayer did Jacob refer to him as "my God" (cf. 28:21). Greater faithfulness remained for the patriarch.

Following his prayer, Jacob sent to Esau 550 animals (not counting the young), divided into their respective herds. He ordered his servants to present them to Esau in such a way that the escalating nature of the gifts would overwhelm his brother. Jacob's plan, which seems to have been very sincere, had the vibes of both a sacrifice to placate wrath and tribute paid to a king (cf. "appease," "present," vv. 20-21). Jacob knew this wasn't the time to be stingy; he wanted to overwhelm his brother with generosity.

Read Genesis 32:22-32. While Jacob's servants drove the herds toward Esau, Jacob transported his family to the north bank of the Jabbok River. The Jabbok's course cuts a deep canyon before it joins the Jordan, so crossing this river in the middle of the night would have been a rather precarious undertaking. But Jacob did so because, at this point, he was anxious and desperate. With nothing more than a river standing between his family and his brother, Jacob settled in for the night—until a visitor appeared.

The identity of this visitor is still a mystery. He is called a "man" throughout the story, "God" in vv. 28, 30, and an "angel" in Hos. 12:4. It's also possible that Jacob encountered the pre-incarnate Christ. Whatever the exact identity of this visitor, it is clear that Jacob encountered God in some form.

Not surprisingly, Jacob's request for his assailant's name was ignored. Instead, the midnight visitor asked for Jacob's name, not because he didn't know, but because he wanted Jacob to confess that he had been "the Deceiver" all his life. A new name was then conferred upon the patriarch, and the sun rose on a changed Jacob. Not insignificantly, the mysterious visitor says Jacob had "prevailed" (v. 28) in this struggle with God and man. In other words, he had finally come to grips with his "Grabber" ethos, with his penchant to trick and deceive in order to provide. His new name held the promise of a new future. And if the night needed to become even more remarkable, Jacob suddenly realized it had been God with whom he had wrestled (v. 30). And if Jacob had struggled with God and survived, he need not fear his reunion with Esau.

The narrator makes one final note before shifting to the next scene. We are told that ancient Israel did not eat "the sinew of the thigh that is on the hip socket" (v. 32). This ban on eating that part of an animal is not mentioned again in the Old Testament, though it does show up in certain rabbinical writings.

Read Genesis 33. Having come to terms with God by very dramatic means, Jacob faced the next day with a little less anxiety. As Esau and his entourage approached, Jacob grouped his wives and children in preparation for the reunion. And while the 400 men are again mentioned (v. 1), Jacob does not seem as panicked as he had been the day before (32:7-8).

In keeping with his overtones of "lord" and "servant," Jacob bowed prone to Esau seven times out of respect. However, the pain of past injustices had faded from Esau's mind; he ran to hug his brother, and both men wept as they embraced each other for the first time in many years. Jacob introduced his brother to his wives and twelve children. When Esau inquired about the herds that had been brought to him the previous day, Jacob explained they were intended as a gift meant to please Esau (v. 8). Esau protested that such gifts were unnecessary, but Jacob further insisted that Esau accept them, perhaps to recompense his brother for stealing his birthright.

There is no doubt the events of the previous night were on Jacob's mind as he embraced his brother. He told Esau that seeing him was "like seeing the face of God" (v. 10; cf. 32:30). In Esau's forgiveness, Jacob noticed a reflection of the mercy God had extended to him the previous night. The patriarch also knew it was only by the protection and providence of God that Esau had not attacked with vindictive fury.

Esau offered to travel with Jacob to provide protection, but Jacob politely refused his brother's offer. His stated reason was that travel with women, children, and young livestock would be slow. When Esau offered to leave some of his men behind to assist, Jacob again refused and promised to continue towards Esau's home in Edom. Jacob was intent on settling down elsewhere.

Jacob's family made their home at Succoth, a location on the east bank of the Jordan near its confluence with the Jabbok. In this very fertile area, Jacob remained for a while. He then moved on to the outskirts of Shechem, a city 35 miles north of Jerusalem, where he purchased property. This property would become Joseph's final resting place (Josh. 24:32), and Jacob built an altar here in worship to God, just as his grandfather Abraham had done decades before (12:6). This act was a significant one because unlike his prayer in 32:9-12, Jacob here makes his relationship with God a personal one, calling him "God, the God of Israel."

APPLICATION

Fear & Faith. One scholar astutely notes, "Jacob's life is laced with fear." He was fearful of his dream at Bethel (28:17), fearful of Laban (31:31), and fearful of Esau (32:7). This is the unavoidable end of the self-sufficient man: fear. Anxiety and worry are the fruit of not trusting in God. Over and over, the Bible calls the people of God to exchange their fear for faith. And over and over, we see the victories faith can deliver when fear would have collapsed into inglorious destruction. The reason self-sufficiency breeds fear is because our own strength will eventually fail us (Isa. 40:30). It is inevitable that our best won't be good enough. And the failures of the past cause us to fear the challenges and unknowns of the future. The only way our fear can give way to faith is to trust in God's perfect love that casts out fear (1 John 4:18).

Breaking Bad Habits. Jacob's penchant for self-sufficiency was borderline pathological. He sought blessing and success through his own efforts. But this had blown up in his face, destroying his relationships with Esau and Laban. There is a release when we invest our faith and confidence in the promises of God and in heeding God's call to get out of our own way. If necessary, God will be both relentless and ruthless in expelling self-sufficiency from our hearts. As he did with Jacob, he will go as far as to "cripple" us if doing so makes us lean harder on him. He will bring us to the very point of death if it helps us trust him more (2 Cor. 1:9; 12:7-10).

Give & Take. Jacob's wrestling match with God was a watershed moment. All his life, Jacob had practiced a profane self-sufficiency. Before his birth, great things had been forecasted for him (25:23), but Jacob had swindled Esau out of his birthright and deceived his father in order to receive the blessing. He who had been hoodwinked by his uncle (29:23) had turned the deception back onto Laban (30:25-43). Even his parting request for a blessing and his assailant's name (32:29) was a last-ditch effort to regain some control. Jacob was seeking to manipulate a situation in which he had no advantage. Such behavior makes blessings appear to be the product of our striving, rather than evidence of the great mercy and amazing grace of God. We can't experience fully the warm embrace of grace until we have allowed God to break us of our self-sufficiency.

CONCLUSION

The disaster with Esau had been averted, and Jacob was now a faithful servant of the living God after surviving his midnight wrestling match. But more problems lay ahead for Jacob's family. As we will discover in the next chapter, spiritual restoration does not always trigger personal success or family harmony. But for now, we should appreciate the progress Jacob has made in his spiritual development. As he limped away from his experience with God and Esau on the banks of the Jabbok, every painful step was a testimony to the sovereign Authorship of his life's story.

QUESTIONS FOR REFLECTION

1. Why did Jacob send advance messengers to Esau before the meeting?

2. The messengers reported that Esau was headed Jacob's way with 400 men. Why was this number ominous?

3. What was Jacob's response to this threat? In what ways was it a departure from his past behavior?

4. Though the exact identity is elusive, Jacob encountered whom on the banks of the Jabbok?

5. What gift of God does self-sufficiency prevent us from fully and warmly embracing?

QUESTIONS FOR DISCUSSION

1. Describe Jacob's attitude and posture towards Esau in this lesson. Why did he act this way?

2. How did the midnight wrestling match fortify Jacob for meeting Esau?

3. How is Jacob's reconciliation with Esau a mirror of his reconciliation with God?

4. How does self-sufficiency breed fear? How does submission and obedience breed faith?

5. In what ways has God "crippled" you to break you of self-sufficiency and teach you to trust in him?

6

JACOB & HIS FAMILY

GENESIS 34-36

Objective: To evaluate Jacob's spiritual leadership of his family

INTRODUCTION

After his reconciliation with Esau, the focus slowly shifts to the lives of Jacob's children, but not before recounting his return to Bethel in order to fulfill his vow to God. The birth of Benjamin, the deaths of Deborah, Rachel, and Isaac, and the descendants of Esau are all discussed in this section. There's a lot that goes on here, and these events can be difficult to digest. What are we to make of the massacre of Shechem? And what of Reuben committing adultery with his father's concubine? In all of these events, both good and bad, God continued to work out his plan to redeem the world.

EXAMINATION

Read Genesis 34. Over the years since his reunion with Esau, Jacob's daughter Dinah grew into a young woman. While away visiting friends, the son of the area ruler raped her. Yet in its aftermath, Shechem fell in love with and wanted to marry Dinah, so he asked his father to make the arrangements. Jacob and his sons were approached with the proposition, although they already knew of the rape. Shechem and his father offered no apology and pretended they did not have Dinah locked up in the city. Shechem offered to pay whatever bride price was demanded. Jacob's sons agreed to the marriage proposal on the condition that the area men become circumcised. The narrator carefully notes this condition was merely a ploy to mask their real plans (v. 13).

The deal, however, had to be ratified by all the men of the area, and such was done at an impromptu meeting. The men agreed to the mandated circumcision. While they were recovering from the surgery, one that was painful and debilitating for several days, Simeon and Levi attacked the city. The other sons of Jacob plundered the town, but Simeon and Levi were focused solely on avenging their sister. Jacob angrily confronted them both when they returned, claiming they had jeopardized their family's peaceful existence in the area; the patriarch later recalled the incident on his deathbed, cursing his sons' violent overreaction (49:5-7).

This story is admittedly difficult to interpret for several reasons. The original audience would have read the narrative in light of the Old Testament's "eye for an eye" doctrine (Exod. 21:23-25), but Christians must now study it through the lens of Jesus' teaching concerning revenge and forgiveness (Matt. 5:38-42; 18:21-35). Jacob was furious that his sons had resorted to violence, though one wonders why he wasn't so grieved when he learned his daughter had been raped. In fact, I think Jacob was angrier at how Simeon and Levi had left the family vulnerable (v. 30) than he was over their deception. To complicate matters further, the Lord mitigated Jacob's fear of retaliation by striking fear in the hearts of area inhabitants (35:5). What, then, is to be gained from this story?

On an individual level, we can absolutely and definitely say it is always wrong to seek revenge—that belongs to God alone (Rom. 12:19). It requires remarkable trust to forgive a sin similar to the one Shechem committed, but this is the only way for Christians to live. And while forgiveness may be difficult to extend in the immediate aftermath of a crime, it must be extended at some point, and sooner rather than later, lest we burn the bridge over which we too must cross (Matt. 6:14-15). In all things, Christians are to consign themselves "to him who judges justly" (1 Pet. 2:23).

However, on a societal level, evil must not be tolerated, but rather punished by neutral parties. Note that Paul's remarks on revenge in Rom. 12

are immediately followed by an endorsement of civil government as God's agent to punish those who violate moral law (Rom. 13:4). This principle was arguably Moses' motive for recording this story. The phrase in v. 7, "he [Shechem] had done an outrageous thing in Israel," makes no sense unless we remember this narrative was preserved for the entire nation of Israel. Perhaps Moses meant for Simeon and Levi's closing words to be a warning to Israel's tribes: if there is sin in the camp, it cannot go unpunished, or the moral fabric of a godly society will quickly unravel (Eccles. 8:11).

Read Genesis 35. At God's command, Jacob left the area of Shechem and journeyed to Bethel. This had been the place where he had previously vowed his allegiance to God if he were protected on his flight from Esau (28:18-22). God had indeed been with Jacob since that time, and now that he was about to return to this sacred place, Jacob ordered his family to cast out all the pagan objects in their possession and purify themselves.

It's clear in the text that God protected Jacob's family from retribution for the Shechem massacre; "a terror from God fell upon the cities that were around them" (v. 5). Regardless of whether God approved of Simeon and Levi's act, he had sworn to protect the patriarchs, and God is always faithful to his promises.

Jacob's rededication to the Lord was followed by three deaths. While the family was at Bethel, his mother's nurse died and was buried there (v. 8). We can only speculate as to why notice of Deborah's death is given when we are never told of the deaths of Rebekah or Leah. One possibility is that Deborah represented Jacob's final connection to the pagan culture of Mesopotamia, the homeland of his grandfather Abraham, his mother Rebekah, and other relatives. With all ties now severed, the family of Israel was now free to become exclusively monotheistic.

While at Bethel, God appeared to Jacob and reaffirmed several elements of the Abrahamic covenant, including Jacob's prior name change to Israel, the promise that Jacob's lineage would produce a nation with kings, and the promise of land. It is to the praise of his glory that we serve a God who is not content with making promises once and never mentioning them again, but instead regularly reaffirms his covenant with us. He does so, lest we forget that his faithfulness reaches to the skies (Psa. 57:10).

As the family traveled from Bethel, Rachel gave birth to Jacob's twelfth son. But the woman who had cried to her husband, "Give me children, or I shall die!" (30:1), died tragically in childbirth. Rachel's last words bestowed on the child the name Ben-Oni, meaning "son of my sorrow." But Jacob renamed the child Benjamin. The meaning of Benjamin is debated, being variously interpreted as "son of my right hand" or "son of the south." The third option is to interpret Benjamin as "son of my old age." This may have been Jacob's understanding of the name's meaning (cf. 44:20). Following the death of his beloved wife, Jacob buried Rachel in a tomb near Bethlehem, a landmark that remained famous centuries later (1 Sam. 10:2).

After Rachel's death, Reuben slept with Bilhah, his father's concubine and Rachel's servant. The narrator does not tell us why he committed such an atrocity, but the most reasonable explanation is that Reuben intended to usurp his father's position as leader of the clan (cf. 2 Sam. 3:7-8; 12:7-8; 16:21-22). Reuben's act is referenced later as the reason why the firstborn's birthright was given to Joseph's sons instead (cf. 49:3-4; 1 Chr 5:1). So if Reuben did this to usurp his father's authority and establish himself as clan leader, he failed miserably.

The chapter ends by narrating Isaac's death, though chronologically Isaac wouldn't die until Joseph had been in Egypt for a dozen years. The narrator is clearing the way for Joseph by effectively shuffling Isaac, then Esau, off the stage. Notice that, like his father Abraham, Isaac "died and was gathered to his people, old and full of days" (v. 29, cf. 25:8). And as he and Ishmael had reunited to honor their father in burial, so also Jacob and Esau came together to honor theirs by interring him in the family cemetery.

Read Genesis 36. While still in the womb, God had promised that Esau's lineage would become a nation (25:23). Later, Isaac further expounded on Esau's violent nature and inferiority to Jacob (27:39-40), but God had vowed to make Esau into a nation, and this chapter details how that promise materialized.

Esau and his family settled in the cliffs and plateaus of Seir, an area southwest of the Dead Sea, and this region would become the Edomites' ancestral lands. Esau didn't move away from Jacob because of lingering resentment, but of a true lack of real estate (vv. 6-7). If you see in this an echo of Lot leaving Canaan because there wasn't enough room (13:5-12), you're correct. We are learning that, as far as Genesis is concerned, there is only room enough in the Promised Land for heirs of the Abrahamic covenant (cf. 37:1). But God was also looking out for Edom: the nation of Israel was later commanded to treat Edom as family, and not to confiscate their land, because God had reserved it for Esau's posterity (Deut. 2:5; Josh. 24:4), just as Canaan had been reserved for Abraham, Isaac, and Jacob.

Included in the list of Esau's family tree are a few persons of interest. Born to Esau's son Eliphaz was Amalek (v. 12). His descendants are well known as some of Israel's bitterest enemies (cf. Exod. 17:8-16; Num. 14:45; 1 Sam. 15:1-9). Also of interest in Esau's lineage is his grandson Teman (v. 11); one of Job's three friends was "Eliphaz the Temanite" (Job 2:11).

And then there is mention of Anah, a Horite "who found the hot springs in the wilderness, as he pastured the donkeys of Zibeon his father" (v. 24), a reference to a legend that is now unknown. The translation "hot springs" is based on the Latin Vulgate; Jewish tradition translated the Hebrew phrase as "mules," making Anah the first to crossbreed horses with donkeys and produce the mule. But this doesn't seem to be based on anything more than the similarity between the Hebrew *ha yemim* and the Greek *hemionos* (mules). Others suggest that Anah thought he saw "lakes" in the desert when it was just a mirage, and that the joke is lost on later readers. Genesis sometimes alludes to traditions known to the original audience, but that have since been lost to us.

APPLICATION

Spiritual Leadership in the Home. Quite a troubling development in these chapters is Jacob's loss of control over his family. Beginning in Gen. 34, he failed to respond appropriately to Dinah's rape and was equally unable to restrain his sons from retribution. In Gen. 35, his oldest son threatened his leadership of the clan by sleeping with Bilhah. In coming chapters, Jacob would watch helplessly as his family fractured even further; his sons' hatred towards Joseph climaxed in the latter being sold into slavery. This is not the first time we have seen the breakdown of male leadership in Genesis. The importance of strong spiritual leadership is apparent when it is absent. One of the greatest benefits of strong and sound leadership is that it can prevent tendencies toward excess; i.e. it has a mellowing effect on human sinfulness. This fact influences how Christians choose their leaders and how Christian leadership is exercised. We are to prefer, as well as strive to be, leaders who exercise moderation (cf. the qualifications for elders in 1 Tim. 3:2-7). If we fail in this endeavor, balance will be swallowed up by extremes, and we can expect a lot of unnecessary trouble (Prov. 25:16).

A Failure? It seems quite strange that Jacob's family was not yet monotheistic, but we must concede that Jacob was never the strongest spiritual leader. It is a sad thing when men prove to be ineffective leaders of their families. But just because a man has proven to be an ineffective leader does not make him a poor Christian. The latter portions of Genesis portray Jacob as having little control over his sons, but as Gen. 32 and 35 bears out, he nonetheless sought renewal in his walk with the God of his fathers. When Jacob demanded his family surrender their false gods, they complied. No man or woman can be called a failure who seeks first God's kingdom and his righteousness (Matt. 6:33).

Holy Living. Separation from the world is difficult. Some have tried to separate themselves from the world (e.g. Amish, Mennonites), but tales of sexual abuse and other crimes committed in Amish and Mennonite communities remind us of the harsh reality that "the whole world lies in the power of the evil one" (1 John 5:19). In the wake of the Shechem massacre, perhaps Jacob hoped that, by asking his family to surrender their false gods, such would lead to their leading a holier lifestyle. But such hopes were dashed when Reuben committed his sin. Spiritual renewal and separation from the world is a process that takes place in the inner man. I must be careful about the people with whom I associate, the media I consume, and the places I visit (cf. Phil. 4:8). But the New Testament increasingly speaks of putting away via baptism the sinful desires of the inner self and replacing them with the power of God's Word (cf. Eph. 4:22-25; Col. 3:7-8; Tit. 3:5; Jas. 1:21; 1 Pet. 2:1-2).

CONCLUSION

Here, the narrative closes the books on Isaac and Esau. Even Jacob will now take a backseat, while his sons are thrust onto Genesis' center stage. We have learned much from Jacob, including what happens to people who grab and deceive their way into success instead of trusting God. But Jacob has come a long way. He now trusts God and is faithful to him. Meanwhile, we are about to see how God demonstrated his remarkable faithfulness to another generation of Abraham's offspring.

QUESTIONS FOR REFLECTION

1. Were Dinah's brothers sincere in their proposal to Shechem or was it a ploy? How do you know?

2. What motive did Simeon and Levi have to insist that the men of Shechem be circumcised?

3. How did God protect Jacob in the aftermath of the Shechem massacre?

4. What did Jacob do to rededicate himself to the Lord?

5. What does the name Benjamin mean?

6. How was Reuben's act a challenge to his father's authority?

7. What race/nation of people descended from Esau?

QUESTIONS FOR DISCUSSION

1. In the disagreement of Jacob vs. Simeon and Levi, who was in the right? Why?

2. In your opinion, why was the story of Dinah's rape preserved both for Israel and for us?

3. What are the benefits of strong spiritual leadership, both in the home and the church?

4. What excesses have you seen due to a lack of strong, sound spiritual leadership?

5. Is it practical to isolate ourselves from the world? Why/why not? If it isn't possible, what alternatives do Christians have to live a holy life before God in the midst of a corrupt culture?

7

JOSEPH & HIS BROTHERS

GENESIS 37

Objective: To discover how Joseph's misfortune was really the beginning of God's plan to preserve Israel

INTRODUCTION

No star shines as brightly on the pages of Genesis as Joseph arguably does. Joseph's story captivates us so because he rose above the worst circumstances to become second-in-command of a dominant world power while maintaining remarkable perspective. In many ways, Joseph serves as the perfect climax for Genesis. Unlike those before him, he was willing at an early age to completely surrender his life to God's control. If anyone had the right to abandon faith and morality, it was Joseph. But even as a slave, he acted out his faith in the God of his fathers. The failures of faith that had plagued Abraham, Isaac, and Jacob are strangely absent from Joseph's story, and his circumstances were arguably the most difficult. Thus we are given a glimpse at the very faith and perseverance God wishes for all of us.

EXAMINATION

Read Genesis 37. As the Joseph story commences, we're left with the impression that he was a bratty, bragging tattletale. The text says he carried "a bad report" to Jacob about Dan, Naphtali, Gad, and Asher. Due to this and the special coat given to Joseph, his brothers "hated him and could not speak peacefully to him" (v. 4). And this wasn't "hate" in the sense of our own colloquial, rather flippant, expression. Claus Westermann explains:

> When we use the word "hate," we usually mean something that is a personal position or attitude. However, in the Hebrew, the verb "to hate" has a different meaning: it is a deed or the inception of a deed. To practice this kind of hate is like pulling a bowstring taut — it has no purpose unless an arrow is then unleashed. By the same token, hate makes no sense unless one follows through with a corresponding deed. ... Thus, when our storyteller says that the brothers hated Joseph, we should expect that a hatefulfilling deed will follow.

The favoritism that had plagued Isaac and Rebekah continued with Jacob. He had favored Rachel over Leah and now favored Joseph over his other sons. Though Joseph was the next-to-youngest, Jacob gave him a special coat. The translation "coat of many colours" (v. 3 KJV) originated in the Septuagint and has become a church- and pop-cultural icon. But this translation has been mostly abandoned in favor of phrases like "ornate robe" and "long robe with sleeves." Whatever its physical appearance, it was surely a garment that only the very wealthy could afford.

And we can imagine that the dreams didn't help either. In one, sheaves of grain that had been bound by Joseph's brothers bow down to Joseph's sheaf of grain, indicative that Joseph would one day reign over his brothers. Twice it is said, both before and after the account of the dream, that his brothers "hated him even more" (vv. 5, 8). In the second dream, the sun, moon, and eleven stars bowed to him. This particular dream invited further hatred, as well as Jacob's stern reprimand, but he also "kept the saying in mind" (v. 11).

The next scene of the story happened sometime later. Joseph was sent by Jacob fifty miles north to Shechem to check on his brothers and the family flocks (when he bid Joseph farewell that day, he had no idea that he would not see his favorite son for more than twenty years). Jacob's anxiety no doubt had something to do with the massacre that had happened at Shechem only a few years before (Gen. 34). When the brothers were not at Shechem as expected, Joseph, off of a tip, headed some fifteen miles farther north to Dothan.

Joseph's brothers saw him coming from quite a ways; they no doubt easily identified him from a long distance by his unique coat. They snidely called him "this dreamer" (v. 19). The special coat Joseph wore was a source of consternation, but it seems the dreams had been the final straw. They hated their brother to the point that they wanted to be rid of him by any means necessary. What the brothers wanted to do to Joseph is what Cain had done to Abel. They didn't intend to club Joseph "accidentally" over the head, but to brutally murder him in a gruesome, grizzly manner. As was the case with Cain, the fact that Joseph's brothers were willing to commit fratricide exposes the depths of their depravity.

Reuben, however, comes to Joseph's defense. He convinces his brothers to throw Joseph into a cistern, but not to take his life. The narrator then lets us in on the fact that Reuben intended to "rescue him out of their hand to restore him to his father" (v. 22). Reuben could have wanted to save Joseph because he felt some affection for his little brother, but he might have also been motivated by a desire to restore himself to his father's good graces after his previous indiscretion (35:22).

As soon as Joseph arrived, he was stripped of the symbol of his father's favoritism and thrown into a cistern. Joseph's brothers may have intended to leave Joseph in the pit indefinitely and allow him to die from thirst, starvation, exposure to the elements, a wild animal, or whatever else might happen by chance. It's quite certain that they were callously indifferent to Joseph's cries for help (cf. 42:21) as they sat down to their meal.

While they were eating, it "just so happened" that a caravan passed their way. It seems coincidental or bad luck for Joseph, but it wasn't. Dothan sat on a major trade route, the Via Maris, that ran all the way to Egypt. So, as John Walton reminds us, "it is no surprise that a caravan should pass that way, but the timing is providential." The narrator wants us to pick up on the fact that very few details in Joseph's story—the dreams, the anonymous tipster, the caravan—are coincidental. Every specific of Joseph's life was unfolding under the sovereign watch of a loving God who was orchestrating his plan to preserve the world from a deadly famine.

When Judah saw the caravan on the horizon, he suggested the brothers would better profit from selling Joseph into slavery instead of murdering him. He hoped his reasoning, "for he is our brother, our own flesh" (v. 27), would make him appear humane and merciful. But while some may see the brothers' selling Joseph as a more humane alternative to murder, the original audience may not have agreed. In that time, people were commonly sold into slavery in Egypt as punishment for various crimes, including defaulting on debts. The demand for slaves became so high that people began kidnapping others and profiting from their sale, so legislation sprang up in ancient Near Eastern societies to squelch this morally horrific act. The Law of Moses made kidnapping and selling someone into slavery a capital offense (Exod. 21:16; Deut. 24:7). Nonetheless, hatred and greed make cozy bedfellows. Since ten shekels was an annual salary for a day laborer of that time, each brother stood to make several thousand dollars in today's money off the sale of their brother.

When Reuben discovered Joseph was no longer in the pit, he became visibly and sincerely upset. Meanwhile, the brothers devised a scheme to deceive Jacob concerning Joseph's fate. They would show him the precious coat—torn and blood-soaked—and allow him to draw his own conclusions. The depth of their heartless indifference is seen in their use of "your son" instead of "our brother."

In response, Jacob "tore his garments and put sackcloth on his loins and mourned for his son many days" (v. 34). Jacob's grief was inconsolable; no one could comfort him, for he had resigned himself to spend the rest of his days mourning his son's presumed death.

The final verse of Gen. 37 informs us of what happened to Joseph while his father mourned his "death." He was sold as a slave to a man named Potiphar, whom the text calls "an officer of Pharaoh, the captain of the guard" (v. 36). Whatever the scope of Potiphar's responsibilities, it is certain that he exercised oversight over the prison (40:3-4; 41:10, 12).

APPLICATION

The Dreamer. Joseph's dreams are powerful indicators that God was directing the events of Joseph's life just as he had for Joseph's ancestors. What others may consider to have been luck, karma, or coincidence is made clear in the Joseph story to be the providence of God. In these dreams, the Lord gave to Joseph a vision (yet unclear) of the course his life would take, and at every juncture in the narrative is a reminder that the story is unfolding according to God's plan. Nothing was left to fate. And though God no longer reveals his will or plan to us via dreams, it remains nonetheless true that nothing in our lives is left to fate. Rather, God directs our steps (Prov. 16:9; Jer. 10:23).

The What-if Game. Was it only coincidence that Joseph ran into the anonymous tipster at Shechem (whom ancient rabbis identified as an angel) who told of his brothers' new location? Imagine how the course of Joseph's life would have been different if he had returned home to Jacob and reported: "I couldn't find them." When tragedy strikes, we often play the what-if game, but it is not healthy, nor does it deepen our faith. The story of Joseph is a testimony to the fact that God is greater than the dark powers; he can and will work all things for our good and his glory (Rom. 8:28; 11:36). When we find ourselves in the throes of suffering and pain, we must refuse to play the what-if game. Ask instead, "What if God is greater than my current circumstances? If God is indeed working out a plan to bring himself greater glory, how should I react?" Then respond accordingly, confident that he can use our disappointment to deepen our faith.

CONCLUSION

As a child, I enjoyed reading books that offered a "Create your own adventure." At the bottom of the page, you were presented with a choice. Does the hero go into the dark cave or run to safety? Does the general order his troops into battle or retreat and live to fight another day? Does the captain sail one more day in search of buried treasure or return to a safe port? Your decision determined which page you turned to, and the adventure continued to unfold based on more decisions.

Throughout the twists and turns of life, it is often tempting to think of life as simply a series of choices that we make and nothing more. To be sure, human responsibility has a great deal to do with how our lives unfold. But instead of always second-guessing our decisions, wishing we could go back and "choose another page," we must make the decision we believe best honors the Lord and trust that he will direct our steps. Confidence in God's providential plan is crucial in life. Joseph may have second-guessed many of his decisions as he languished in Egypt. Little did he know, however, that God would preserve his family as a result of Joseph's (and his brothers') choices.

QUESTIONS FOR REFLECTION

1. The text says that his brothers "hated" Joseph. Is this different from our common understanding of "hate"? If so, how?

2. What did Joseph's "coat of many colors" actually signify? Why was it a source of his brothers' jealousy?

3. When they saw him coming, what did the brothers initially plan to do to him? Who intervened initially? What alternative did he propose? Why?

4. Which brother suggested selling Joseph into slavery? Why do you think the other brothers heeded his advice and not Reuben's?

5. Was selling Joseph into slavery a more humane alternative than murder? Why/why not?

QUESTIONS FOR DISCUSSION

1. In your opinion, does Joseph make a favorable impression at the beginning of Gen. 37? Explain your answer.

2. What motive did Reuben have for attempting to save Joseph from harm?

3. List the "coincidences" in this story. How are they actually evidence of God's providence?

4. Have you been tempted to play the "What if?" game in the aftermath of tragedy? How so? Did it help you heal?

5. Given the choice between playing "What if?" and trusting God's plan, which would you choose? Why?

8

JUDAH & TAMAR

GENESIS 38

Objective: To understand this story's connection to the Joseph narrative and why it was preserved in Scripture

INTRODUCTION

Ever so often in Scripture, we stumble on a story that is as bizarre and confusing as it is unexpected. The story of Judah and Tamar in Gen. 38 is one of those stories. This is arguably the most difficult chapter in Genesis to interpret, and for many good reasons. If the scandalous nature of its contents doesn't make it difficult, its placement sure does. One has to wonder why such a bizarre story about Judah is placed in the middle of the *Joseph* narrative. The end of the previous chapter left us all wondering what would become of Joseph in Egypt. So why must this chapter come along and ruin the flow of the narrative?

EXAMINATION

Read Genesis 38. This bizarre chapter commences with brief details of Judah's marriage to a Canaanite woman, an event that must have agitated his father as it had Isaac (26:35; 28:1) and frightened Abraham (24:3). The narrator certainly seems to have not approved since he never mentioned the woman's name.

Judah's oldest son, Er, married a woman named Tamar, but the Lord put him to death because of some unexplained sin. As was expected in that culture, if the deceased had no children, an unmarried brother was required to provide an heir for his brother. But Onan, Judah's middle child, had no intention of doing so (cf. Deut. 25:5-10). As the oldest surviving son, he stood to inherit two-thirds of Judah's estate. But if an heir for Er were fathered, Onan would have been left with only a fourth. So to prevent this, Onan would ejaculate on the ground during intercourse. This was not a one-time thing; the use of "whenever" (v. 9) indicates Onan did this repeatedly, and it angered God because it showed scorn for his deceased brother and was a violation of his levirate obligations. As a result, God killed him.

Judah's youngest son was not yet marrying age, so Judah sent Tamar back to her father with the promise that Shelah would one day be her husband when he was old enough. But Judah had no intention of keeping his promise. He may have believed the death of his sons was punishment from God for how he had (recently?) treated Joseph. That, or he simply believed Tamar was cursed; becoming a quick widow in two successive marriages would raise a few questions with anyone. Years later, it became evident that Judah had lied to Tamar, so she devised a plan to become pregnant and provide an heir for Er. Tamar's plan was wholly consistent with the custom of the day that called for a widow to marry her husband's father if her husband's brother died without providing an heir.

"In the course of time" (v. 12), Judah journeyed to Timnah to shear sheep. This event was often accompanied by raucous celebration and inebriation (cf. 1 Sam. 25:4, 36; 2 Sam. 13:23, 28). Presumably under both the influence of alcohol and the impression that Tamar was a random prostitute, Judah solicited her, promising her later payment. As a "pledge" or collateral, Tamar insisted that Judah temporarily forfeit his signet ("seal" NIV), cord, and staff (cf. Num. 17:2)—which would equate to someone's driver's license and credit cards today. Tamar now had undeniable evidence to later prove Judah's identity.

When Judah sent payment to the prostitute, she was nowhere to be found, so he assumed the incident was closed until he received word from his daughter-in-law three months later that she was pregnant. Believing that she had become so illegitimately (she had), he swore that he would execute her by having her burned alive, a sentence that was unusually cruel since stoning would have been more common (Deut. 22:20-24). Tamar countered Judah's oath by producing his seal, cord, and staff, dramatically declaring that the owner had impregnated her. To his credit, Judah instantly recognized that he had forced Tamar into these circumstances by not honoring his word. His statement, "She is more righteous than I" (v. 26), was an admission that Tamar's priorities—perpetuating the covenant family of Abraham—were greater than his own.

So what connection does this story have with Joseph? And why in the world was it preserved for us in Scripture? Nothing in the Bible is arranged by accident, and this salacious story actually has several connections with Gen. 37. It also portends what is to come in the Joseph narrative. Anyone who has seen films directed by M. Night Shyamalan will understand this principle. In his films, certain details and objects cryptically augur future developments (e.g. the half-empty water glasses in *Signs*, the red-hooded costume in *The Village*). In Gen. 38, several details in Judah's life either hearken back to or foreshadow events in Joseph's:

- In the narratives of Gen. 37-38, both stories have a goat at the center (37:31; 38:17, 20), and both turn on a dramatic identification of Joseph/Judah using their respective personal items (cf. 37:32; 38:25), a twist that will occur again in the next chapter (39:13-18).

- God's preference for the younger over the older is again put on display. Perez defied the odds and "broke out" before his older brother. Joseph would defy the odds and "break out" over his brothers, as would Judah over Reuben, and Ephraim over Manasseh.

- In Gen. 38, Judah succumbed to sexual temptation. In the next chapter, Joseph resisted it.

- The most important principle of this chapter is one that will become the central theme of Joseph's story as well: God transforms evil into good to further his purposes (45:5-8; 50:20). One might argue that this is among the most prominent themes in Scripture, for Christ descended from Judah through Perez (Matt 1:3), and it was the deeds of evil men that led providentially to the salvation of the world (Acts 4:27-28).

In the final analysis, this chapter informs us that Judah is on a spiritual journey of his own. Tamar's revelation and Judah's subsequent humiliation occurred after Joseph had been sold into slavery, so this story may be the reason why the Judah of Gen. 43-44 seems kinder and gentler than the one in Gen. 37. Rough and calloused, he had sold his little brother into slavery and was willing to see his daughter-in-law burned for her sexual immorality. But when challenged, he owned and confessed his sin (v. 26). From this point forward, Judah was painfully conscious of his father's grief, and his transformation into a righteous family leader arguably began with his confession.

APPLICATION

The Judah Saga. Until the end of this story, Judah seems to be an apple that never rolled far from the tree. He exhibits all the selfish, dehumanizing traits of his father (Jacob) and grandfather (Laban). Little, if anything, seems redeemable in Judah until Tamar confronts him with his hypocrisy (and in more ways than one!). But this story marks the beginning of a transformation in Judah's character. Later in Joseph's story, we see a more compassionate Judah take center stage. Genesis will end with Judah receiving a significant blessing from his father; his tribe will grow to dominate Israel. Judah will even father Israel's greatest king (David), to say nothing of her Savior. Judah, then, is testimony to God's patient pursuit of our hearts. As Paul put it to the Philippians, "he who began a good work in you will bring it to completion at the day of Jesus Christ" (1:6). For anyone who considers themselves "too far gone" to be of any use for God, Judah's saga argues otherwise.

Birth Control. The demise of Onan in this story has often been used as an argument against the use of any and all uses of birth control. It is certainly true that God desires his people to multiply. But to use Onan's death as an argument against birth control misses the point entirely (for one thing, God is powerful enough to open and close wombs at his discretion). Onan was struck down because he refused to perform his legal obligation of fathering a child on behalf of his brother. That he would ejaculate on the ground instead of attempting to conceive with Tamar proves that he saw her as little more than a sex object; he clearly had no qualms with sharing a bed with her, only with being her baby daddy. Onan, then, serves as a warning against the dehumanizing power of lust and sexual immorality.

Enroll the Widows. In Gen. 38, Tamar is made out to be the heroine. Few of her actions are commendable, but she nonetheless emerges as an empathetic figure who deserved better than she received. The Law of Moses would later call for compassionate treatment of widows, and in the New Testament, this concern is reflected in the early church's charitable distributions (Acts 6:1; 1 Tim. 5:9). Admittedly, widows have greater access to resources today than they did in the ancient Near East, but they often still live on a meager fixed income. And regardless of their economic situation, they remain in need of emotional support. There is a connection between the spiritual vibrancy of a church and the level of its concern for widows—not to mention orphans, immigrants, and the poor. Jesus warned that we will be judged on how we treat "the least of these" (Matt. 25:31-46).

CONCLUSION

For rather obvious reasons, this story was omitted from the Sunday School curriculum of my childhood. Its subject matter—from masturbation to prostitution—scarcely merits a "G" rating. But the Word of God never claims to present us with a morally-sanitized version of events. Rather, it deals with real life in all its unsavoriness. In that light, this story clues us in to the resolution of Joseph's story, but also informs us that Jacob's favorite son was not the only brother in whom God was at work for the purposes of his plan and glory.

QUESTIONS FOR REFLECTION

1. Why was Onan reluctant to do his duty as a brother and father a child with Tamar?

2. In your opinion, why did Judah not keep his promise to give his youngest son to Tamar?

3. In ancient times, what significance lay in a man's seal, cord, and staff?

4. When he learned his former daughter-in-law was pregnant, Judah wanted to execute her by what means? What means of execution was more common for adulteresses?

5. What was the meaning of Perez's name?

QUESTIONS FOR DISCUSSION

1. In what ways does Judah's character evolve or transform in this story?

2. What ties exist between this story and the rest of Joseph's story?

3. In your opinion, what purpose did the divine narrator have for recording this story?

4. In what ways does your church minister to widows, particularly their financial and/or emotional needs?

5. When we fellowship with the "least of these" (i.e. widows, orphans), how is it that we also fellowship with Christ?

9

JOSEPH IN EGYPT

GENESIS 39-41

Objective: To observe God's faithfulness to Joseph
during his suffering and triumph in Egypt

INTRODUCTION

The end of Gen. 37 had left us pondering Joseph's fate in Egypt. For all we
knew at the time, he had been left to waste his life as a slave in some household. Heartlessly sold by his brothers, it would be easy for anyone to conclude that God had forsaken Joseph. And as his time in Egypt continues—a
false rape allegation and a forgetful butler—it seems this was the case.

But life's circumstances are a terrible barometer of whether God is
with us. Despite his circumstances, Joseph was very much on God's mind.
Little did he know that God was providentially working Joseph's darkness
into a great blessing—the salvation of Egypt from a catastrophic natural disaster. God's timing is always perfect, and he is always faithful to his people.

EXAMINATION

Read Genesis 39. Purchased by Potiphar as a slave, he subsequently rose to
power because "the LORD was with Joseph" (v. 2), an important phrase that

occurs three additional times in the chapter (vv. 3, 21, 23). Eventually, Joseph became overseer of his master's entire estate, and things went very well.

Scripture hardly ever describes the physical appearance of someone unless it is crucial to the story, and it does so here: "Now Joseph was handsome in form and appearance" (v. 6). His appearance did not escape the eye of Potiphar's wife, who began seducing Joseph and was rebuffed on every occasion. Joseph displayed an appreciation for moral absolutes and explained that accepting her proposition would be a gross abuse of trust, a violation of her marriage vows, and a sin against God (vv. 8-9).

Eventually, Potiphar's wife tried to force herself on Joseph, but he fled from the house, leaving his coat in her hands. The phrase "to do his work" (v. 11) effectively exonerates Joseph from any mischief or wrongdoing; it is clear he was simply going about his regular responsibilities when he was attacked and framed.

Potiphar's wife unleashed a torrent on Joseph for having rejected her. She also accused her husband of having brought Joseph into his employ in order to "laugh" at her (vv. 14, 17). In response to these allegations, Potiphar's "anger was kindled" (v. 19). In prison, Joseph surely must have felt as if he had hit rock bottom in life, but the narrator surprisingly repeats his previous claim: "the LORD was with Joseph" (v. 21). That Joseph somehow escaped a death sentence for attempted rape simply proved God was protecting him in this foreign land. It was in prison that Joseph befriended the prison warden, proved himself a capable manager, and again rose to power in his circle of influence, just as he had in Potiphar's employ (cf. vv. 6, 23).

Read Genesis 40. When Joseph was 28, two important officers in Pharaoh's administration were imprisoned. It is not said what crime they committed, but given their position, it could be that they were implicated somehow in a plot to assassinate the king. The chief cupbearer would have been responsible for tasting the king's food and drink to insure no one tried to poison Pharaoh. The chief baker was almost as important a station since he too was responsible for protecting the king.

While in prison, these two men both had dreams and were distraught that they had no one to explain the meaning. In Egyptian society, dreams were considered an important means used by the gods to communicate with man, especially to foretell future events. As a result, an entire system of dream interpretation sprang up in Egyptian culture. Professional dream interpreters were in Pharaoh's employ. This explains why the cupbearer and baker were so distraught and troubled—they had no access to these professionals and their dream-interpretation manuals.

While Joseph arguably had no idea that this occasion would catapult him from his miserable circumstances, his great faith informed him that the interpretation of these two dreams could only be discerned by God (v. 8), not by consulting "dream books" as was done by Egyptians and Babylonians. After hearing the dreams described, Joseph told the cupbearer that his dream portended his release and restoration in just three days time. When this came to pass, Joseph asked the cupbearer to remember the injustices done to Joseph and to mention his situation to Pharaoh.

The interpretation of the baker's dream was exactly the opposite; in fact, Joseph links the two by saying to each "Pharaoh will lift up your head" (vv. 13, 19), but to the baker he adds the phrase "from you!" In other words, the baker would be beheaded in three days and his corpse impaled on a stake. Hanging was considered a dishonorable death in ancient times (Deut. 21:22-23; Josh. 8:29; 2 Sam. 4:12). Considering the lengths Egypt went to in a quest to preserve the body after death (e.g. mummification), the fact that the birds would pick the baker's carcass clean meant his death would be especially ignoble. In the baker's dream, it was rather ominous that he was unable to drive the birds away, and that detail foreshadowed his fate.

Bizarrely, we are not told how the cupbearer or baker responded to their respective interpretations. But we do know that everything happened just as Joseph predicted—though arguably not as he planned. The cupbearer was restored, and the baker was destroyed. "Yet the chief cupbearer did not remember Joseph, but forgot him" (v. 23). Joseph would languish in prison for two more years.

Read Genesis 41. After two years, Pharaoh had two dreams: the first about seven healthy and unhealthy cows, the second about seven healthy and unhealthy heads of grain, the latter being damaged by the "east wind." These dreams disturbed him because dreams were considered communication from the gods in ancient times, and unlike other dreams in Genesis, Pharaoh was not the central figure. Pharaoh summoned his dream-interpretation specialists, but they were powerless. It was only then that the cupbearer remembered Joseph and his ability to interpret dreams.

Joseph was quickly summoned to Pharaoh's court. He shaved his head and face and changed his clothes. We may think these details only mean that he cleaned up to be presentable at court, but "cleaning up" for a Hebrew did not entail shaving since they wore beards from puberty onwards. When Joseph shaved before appearing in Pharaoh's court, it might have been for the first time ever. So this detail is preserved for us as notice that Joseph was allowing himself to be "Egyptianized" or transformed in a way that would render him unrecognizable to his brothers a few years later.

When Joseph appeared before him, Pharaoh expressed his belief that Joseph was one of these magicians capable of special powers. "I have heard it said of you that when you hear a dream you can interpret it" (v. 15). Joseph's response was stunning and unwise in a context where conventional wisdom dictated the virtues of tooting your own horn. "It is not in me; God will give Pharaoh a favorable answer" (v. 16). In ancient Egypt, Pharaoh considered himself to be a god, so Joseph's response wasn't exactly diplomatic. But Joseph credited the true God of heaven with the revelation because that was the truth, and people of faith speak what is true.

The seven healthy cows/heads of grain were seven years of abundant prosperity, while the seven unhealthy cows/heads of grain were seven years of severe famine. That Pharaoh had two dreams of the same substance demonstrated that God had firmly decreed this to happen, and it would happen soon (v. 32).

Bizarrely, Joseph then proceeded to give his unsolicited advice as to what should be done in order to prepare Egypt for the severe famine. First, Pharaoh should appoint a "wise man" to be in charge. Otherwise, when the famine worsened, food would only go to the influential. Second, he must establish regional overseers. This job was too much for one person. Finally, the nation must collect 20% of the crop yield for the next seven plenteous years and warehouse it for use during the famine. The grain would be sold back to the very people who had contributed it.

Pharaoh recognized Joseph's wisdom, but also that he had been endowed with "the Spirit of God." He made Joseph the second-most powerful person in the country, bestowing him with special privileges and titles in order to fulfill his duties. The signet ring given by Pharaoh allowed Joseph to perform state business in Pharaoh's name. The fine clothes and gold chain likewise designated Joseph as a VIP, and to top it all off, Joseph received his very own chariot complete with runners who acted as an ancient version of the modern-day motorcade filled with Secret Service agents.

The chapter ends by portraying Joseph as enjoying God's lavish blessing and facing the future with great confidence in God. He married into a powerful priestly family in one of ancient Egypt's greatest cities. Joseph also received a new name, the meaning of which was derived from an Egyptian word that meant "the creator/sustainer of life." The Lord blessed him and his wife with two boys, and their names confirmed Joseph's belief that God was with him. Notice that Manasseh and Ephraim are Hebrew names; Joseph had experienced a startling rise to power, but he hadn't forgotten his home or heritage.

APPLICATION

Flee Fornication. It is hard to imagine that Paul didn't have Joseph in mind when he exhorted the Corinthians to "flee from sexual immorality" (1 Cor. 6:18). Once he knew of her desires, Joseph refused to be alone with Potiphar's wife. I find it intriguing and significant that *sexual* temptation is the only kind from which the New Testament admonishes us to flee (2 Tim. 2:22); against all else, we are told to stand firm (1 Pet. 5:9). It is the one temptation that appeals to the most primitive of our desires. Against all else, a will that is empowered by the Spirit of God equips us to stand our ground. But God created our sexual nature with a particular weakness, one that is beautiful in the context of marriage (1 Cor. 7:5), but terrible outside of it. Christians, whether single or married, should exercise extreme caution and wisdom around members of the opposite sex.

God's Perfect Timing. We frail and pathetic humans have a bad habit of gauging God's presence based on our circumstances. When times are great, God seems very close and friendly; when the storm clouds gather, he feels distant and hostile—if we believe in him at all. But veterans of the life of faith know that circumstances are no better a barometer of whether God is with you than overcast skies are proof that the sun has vanished completely. That's what faith is all about—being convicted "of things not seen" (Heb. 11:1; cf. 2 Cor. 5:7). Joseph had no circumstantial reason to believe that God was with him in Egypt. Can someone really enjoy divine favor that has been sold into slavery by his brothers and then framed for rape and thrown into the dungeon? The answer in Genesis is that they can and do, for God had great things in store for Joseph. Even the cupbearer forgetting about Joseph for two years was a part of God's plan. If Pharaoh had known of Joseph before his dream, would Joseph have been given the opportunity to show his worth? So it is in our lives that just when we think that God has abandoned us, we discover that he has been present all along, plotting for our good and his glory.

CONCLUSION

The closing words of Gen. 41, "the famine was severe over all the earth" (v. 57), set the stage for what would happen next. God had been very faithful to Joseph during his rise to power in Egypt. This favorite son of Jacob had not been abandoned to an Egyptian prison. Joseph had overcome. And as Gen. 41 closes, he may have been very content in his settled life, but more challenges awaited him—challenges that would be greater than any he had already faced.

QUESTIONS FOR REFLECTION

1. What important phrase occurs three times in Gen. 39? What is the phrase's significance?

2. What was Joseph's response to the sexual advances of Potiphar's wife? What did he do when she cornered him one day?

3. Why were the butler and baker "troubled" one morning in prison?

4. Why did Joseph shave before his appearance before Pharaoh?

5. To whom did Joseph give credit for dream interpretation? Why is this significant?

6. What was Joseph's official recommendation or plan for dealing with the impending crisis?

QUESTIONS FOR DISCUSSION

1. What command does the New Testament give concerning *sexual* temptations? How is this different from other temptations? Why must our response to sexual temptations be different?

2. Has there been a time in your life when you struggled to believe God was with you? What "evidence" did your circumstances give as to God's presence?

3. As you look back at that season of your life, can you see that God was very much present in your life? Can you see that he was at work for your good and his glory? How so?

4. Seasons of suffering have the potential to drive us *away from* God, but they often drive us *to* God. On the other hand, seasons of success and prosperity have a higher probability of driving us away from God. Why is this?

5. In the text, what significance was there in the names of Joseph's two sons? Why is it important to celebrate God's healing of past hurt and provision of current/future blessing?

10

JOSEPH IN POWER

GENESIS 42-45

Objective: To learn from Joseph's extraordinary
offer of forgiveness to his brothers

INTRODUCTION

One of the great classics of literature is Alexandre Dumas' *The Count of
Monte Cristo*. The story is about a Frenchmen who is wrongly imprisoned
out of jealousy. Left to rot in an island prison, he escapes, finds a priceless
treasure, and lives a life of privilege while seeking revenge on his enemies.

The story has been popular because it feeds our fantasies of what we'd
do if we had the opportunity to get even with the ones who hurt us the
most. In this lesson, we discover that Joseph had the same opportunity, but
passed on vengeance, convinced that such was not consistent for someone
who had tremendous faith in God's providence.

EXAMINATION

Read Genesis 42. As the close of the previous lesson had led us to believe,
the famine indeed affected Canaan. Jacob's question to his sons is comical,
"Why do you look at one another?" (v. 1), but it also underscores the dys-

function of Jacob's family. Upon learning of Joseph's "death," it seems Benjamin had replaced his older brother as his father's favorite son. So when Jacob sent them down to Egypt, he retained Benjamin.

It had been more than twenty years since his brothers had sold Joseph into slavery, so it is not unusual that they did not recognize him. Joseph also had a different name at this point, and in both speech and dress, he would have seemed every bit a native Egyptian. But the hearkening back to Joseph's dreams (v. 9) is an indication to the reader that what is unfolding is from the hand of God. He had given the dreams to Joseph, and he was now fulfilling them as part of his divine plan to save Jacob's family, as well as the whole world.

Much has been speculated regarding Joseph's intentions in Gen. 42-45. Was he punishing his brothers? Teaching them a lesson? Testing them? Did Joseph intend all along for his brothers to spend three days in prison? Did he release them, sans Simeon, because he had a change of heart? The narrator never reveals his thoughts, so we are left with an enigmatic portrayal of Joseph. But if he is anything, Joseph is incredibly shrewd; it seems his plot was an attempt to deduce how Jacob and Benjamin had been treated in his absence. Had his brothers mistreated their father? Had they been as hateful to Benjamin as they had been to Joseph? Why was Benjamin not with the others on this first visit—had they disposed of him as they had Joseph? When Benjamin enjoyed favor at Joseph's banquet (43:34) and received lucrative gifts (45:22), would the brothers be jealous? When the silver cup was found in Benjamin's sack (44:12), would the brothers abandon him to a dungeon in Egypt as they had done Joseph? I think these are the questions to which Joseph sought answers.

Joseph's accusation of espionage (v. 9) wasn't trivial. Spies were common in ancient times, especially when one nation had an apparent advantage over her neighbors during international instability (e.g. a famine). Joseph accused his brothers of trying to locate "the nakedness of the land" or "the undefended parts" of Egypt (NASU). If Egypt's storehouses could be located, they were at risk of being plundered. In response to the accusation, the brothers' rightfully reasoned that no family would risk all of its sons in order to engage in espionage. After three days in prison, the brothers were allowed to leave, but Simeon was kept as collateral until the brothers could produce Benjamin in a return visit. Via his outburst (v. 22), Joseph deduced for the first time that Reuben (the oldest) was not culpable in selling him into slavery, so this may explain why he detained Simeon (the second oldest).

In Joseph's presence, and unaware that he could understand their conversation, the brothers conceded to one another that their misfortune in Egypt was retribution for how they had treated Joseph (v. 21; cf. v. 28; 44:16), "a reckoning for his blood" (v. 22). This will become a recurring theme in the Joseph narrative: the brothers' guilt haunted them, even after their father had passed away (50:15). When his brothers discussed their betrayal before him, Joseph often had to leave the room sobbing (v. 24; 43:30; 45:2).

The nine brothers returned to Canaan with hearts as heavy as their grain sacks. The discovery of their money in the grain sacks was embarrassing; it would have caused their families back at home to assume that the money had either been stolen, or that they had sold Simeon into slavery as they had Joseph two decades before (truth is stranger than fiction). Their worst fears were confirmed when Jacob stubbornly refused to allow Benjamin to make the requisite return journey. And why should he? Twice his sons have returned home less one brother and richer in silver. Why risk Benjamin to such odds? Plus, Jacob's refusal to accept Reuben's offer isn't surprising; why should Jacob trust the son who had such little regard for his father's wife, and appears here to have even less regard for his own sons (v. 37)?

Read Genesis 43. At the end of Gen, 42, we are left wondering about the fate, not only of an incarcerated Simeon, but also of Jacob's entire clan. Their food cannot last forever. Sure enough, it seems an empty stomach changed Jacob's mind, and so he sent his sons to purchase more grain, even including gifts and extra money (vv. 11-12). But convincing Jacob wasn't any easier this time around. He accused his sons of intentionally disclosing Benjamin's existence (v. 6), and Judah had to offer himself as collateral (a more noble act than offering one's two sons) if Benjamin was harmed or didn't return.

Judah is the son who emerges as a leader among his brothers throughout the Joseph narrative. They listened to him when Joseph was sold into slavery. Jacob listened to him here and relinquished Benjamin into his trust, and Judah would be the spokesman in Egypt before Joseph. It might even be said that Judah was developing into a better leader than his father; his statement in v. 10—"If we had not delayed, we would now have returned twice"—is a stinging indictment of Jacob's belligerence that had almost starved the clan.

When his brothers arrived in Egypt, Joseph threw a banquet in their honor, a fact that astonished the Egyptians as much as Joseph's seating his guests per birth-order astonished his brothers. Egyptians of antiquity possessed feelings of racial and religious superiority towards their neighbors. Plus, meats that were staples in the diets of Greeks (beef) and Hebrews (lamb) were sacred to the Egyptians and, therefore, offensive. The Greek historian Herodotus notes that no Egyptian would even go near the eating utensils of the Greeks. This might explain why the Egyptians would not eat with Israel's sons, an act they considered to be "an abomination" (v. 32).

Nonetheless, Joseph's fondness for Benjamin is very clear in the scene. When he met Benjamin, he had to leave the room sobbing (v. 30). At dinner, Benjamin received five times what his brothers received (v. 34). Indeed, Joseph shunned cultural norms and enjoyed a very lively party with all his brothers; the phrase "they drank and were merry with him" means they all got drunk.

Read Genesis 44. After the meal, the brothers were again sent on their way, only to be chased down by Joseph's guards. In response to the accusation that one of them had stolen Joseph's cup, the brothers protested that they could not be dishonest men if they had willingly returned the money from the previous visit (v. 8). But their protests fell on deaf ears. Upon their return, the speech that Judah gave is a rather eloquent one. Much of it rehearses the story so far, an attempt on his part to give the brothers' side of things. Note especially that Judah's opening statement, "God has found out the guilt of your servants" (v. 16), may be a confession of how they had treated Joseph.

But the main thrust of Judah's speech is that if anything happened to Benjamin, it would be the end of Jacob. Judah loved his father, and after seeing Jacob grieve Joseph's "death" the last two decades, Judah was willing to spend the rest of his life in an Egyptian prison if it meant salvaging his father's joy. This is a very different Judah than the one who had sold Joseph into slavery with little regard for how it would affect his father.

Read Genesis 45. Upon hearing Judah's impassioned plea, Joseph yet again "could not control himself" (v. 1) and began sobbing. Clearly, the brothers had a greater love for their father's second-favorite son than they had had for his first. Joseph emptied the room of everyone else except his brothers. This, right here, is the climax of Joseph's entire story. Joseph was in the very position that any emotionally-wounded person would love to be in—to have the opportunity to punish those who have hurt you the most, and with no repercussions whatsoever. No wonder that, when Joseph revealed himself to his brothers, "they were *dismayed* at his presence" (v. 3), a term the Old Testament uses to describe that sickening gut-wrench or paralyzing fear an army has when they realize all hope is lost in battle (Exod. 15:15; Judg. 20:41; Psa. 48:5). Joseph's brothers sensed the Grim Reaper in their midst.

Joseph's speech to his brothers ranks among the most important passages in Scripture. His ability to forgive is as remarkable as was his perspective. He urged his brothers not to wallow in their guilt because God had used their sin to his glory. During his 22 years in Egypt, Joseph had at some point glimpsed the plan of God at work. He understood that his brothers had sinned, but that God had used their sin to deliver many from certain destruction. And because he could see God at work in his suffering, Joseph was able to forgive his brothers' evil act. "God sent me before you to preserve for you a remnant on earth, and to keep alive for you many survivors" (v. 7).

Joseph went so far as to invite his family to move to Egypt so that he could care for them during the remaining years of famine, years in which the famine would reach a greater severity; all agricultural production would reach a devastating halt (v. 6). Pharaoh, out of gratitude to Joseph for his shrewd management of the famine, generously reserved land in Goshen for Jacob and his family, an area located in the northeast portion of the Nile Delta that made for excellent pasture. He also commissioned carts for use in moving the family of Israel from Canaan. In a parting act, Joseph gave his brothers a change of clothes, and to Benjamin five changes of clothes. Jacob had exhibited his favor of Joseph with a special coat. Here, Joseph did the same for his little brother.

The section ends with an aged Jacob, one who thought his only hope was to see his beloved Joseph in Sheol (37:35), learning that Joseph was alive and well. His heart was at first "numb" or hardened to the fact that such could be true, but then his spirit "revived." God had transformed his bitterest heartache into a heartfelt "Hallelujah!"

APPLICATION

The Rise of Judah. While playing a supporting role in the inspired version of *Joseph and the Amazing Technicolor Dreamcoat*, Judah has indeed come a long way. While he exhibits profoundly shady behavior in selling his brother into slavery and denying his daughter-in-law another husband as custom demanded (to say nothing of sleeping with a "prostitute"), Judah evolves into a more mellowed, more compassionate human being and a strong leader. He does the unthinkable in challenging his father's decision regarding Benjamin, and he willingly offers himself up to take Benjamin's place—which likely convinced Joseph that Judah and his brothers had authentically changed. Judah's example, like many others in Scripture, reminds us that God is not through transforming a person's heart until they breathe their last breath. The same redemptive ending that characterized Judah's story can also define our own.

Revenge & Release. In *The Count of Monte Cristo*, the protagonist goes to great lengths to extract revenge on his enemies, foolishly believing that this will make him feel better. Joseph, too, arguably begins a journey down this same road. But whether he was faking initially or simply came to his senses, he models for us the power of forgiveness toward those who have wronged us. Resentment toward those who have hurt us will only breed bitterness, anger, hatred, and—eventually—spiritual death. Resentment grows as we seethe over all the ways that person "owes" us and how we need to get even. But in forgiveness—the Greek term of which literally means "to release"— we turn loose of our bitterness, declaring that the person who wronged us doesn't owe us anymore. We have released them from their debt. There is now no need to get even. Such an attitude admittedly smacks somewhat of injustice, but how can we do anything else in light of what God did for us in Christ (Eph. 4:32)?

Hurt & the Healer. Joseph's perspective, one that was convinced of God's sovereignty over all things, is a model for us to follow. There is no denying that you and I have endured unspeakable hardship. But no matter the severity of our suffering, healing is impossible until we come to grips with this truth: God is sovereign. Whenever God's people are made to suffer at the hands of evil people, we must find a way to surrender our grief to the

Lord and ask that he use it to glorify himself. We must strain to see even the faintest glimmer of God at work in our heartache, for that is the only way the heart can heal. The alternative—shutting God out of our lives because our bitterness is too great—will only lead us down a dark road of despair.

CONCLUSION

Joseph's story is indeed the grand crescendo we have been awaiting in this study of Genesis. Unlike his forefathers, he did not prove unpredictable in his life of faith. And he arguably endured successfully the greatest test ever faced by Abraham or his children. His example affirms that "when we walk with the Lord in the light of his word, what a glory he sheds on our way"!

QUESTIONS FOR REFLECTION

1. Why was Joseph's accusation of espionage a plausible one?

2. What was the brothers' response to this accusation?

3. Who remained behind in Egypt as "collateral" until Benjamin could be brought to Joseph?

4. Which son of Leah becomes a leader among his brothers in these chapters? How so?

5. What was his brothers' reaction when Joseph revealed his true identity?

6. According to Joseph, what was the real cause of his coming to Egypt 22 years before?

QUESTIONS FOR DISCUSSION

1. Is it easy or difficult to believe in God's providence during times of trial? Explain your answer.

2. In your opinion, why did Joseph not reveal himself to his brothers on the first visit?

3. Do you fault Jacob for clinging to Benjamin so stubbornly for so long? Why/why not?

4. Have you ever been in the position where you could extract revenge on someone who hurt you? Did you do so, or did you refuse to take vengeance? Whether you did or didn't, how did your decision make you feel?

5. Explain this statement: "Forgiveness is not for weak people."

11

JOURNEY TO EGYPT

GENESIS 46-47

Objective: To learn how Jacob's family came to live
in Egypt and how God cared for them there

INTRODUCTION

To be an eye-witness to the reunion of Jacob and Joseph would have been a
very special thing. For two decades, Jacob had mourned his favorite son as
lost to death, but God providentially brought them back together.

But the reunion was, to a small degree, bittersweet. Jacob was asked to
leave his home in Canaan and sojourn in Egypt. Granted, Canaan was being ravaged by a famine, and Egypt was the only place in the world that still
had food (due to Joseph's shrewd management!). But Canaan was home.

In this section, we are reminded that God's sovereignty and providential care knows no political boundaries or limitations. God sanctioned
the move to Egypt as his will; he would provide for Israel—in success and
suffering—while they lived in Goshen, just as he had provided for Joseph—
also in success and suffering—while Joseph lived in Pharaoh's shadow.

EXAMINATION

Read Genesis 46. With his entire clan, Jacob moved to Egypt. No one and nothing was left behind because this was not a "Hold the fort down; we'll be back soon" kind of move. At Beersheba, the border of the Promised Land, God appeared to him. Jacob was promised that this move was consistent with God's will—remember that the Lord had previously prohibited Isaac from visiting Egypt during famine (26:2). Jacob may have been apprehensive about the move for this reason, which may also explain why he stopped at Beersheba (the border of Canaan proper) to worship "the God of his father Isaac" (v. 1).

God also affirmed to the patriarch that he would continue to work out his plan to make Abraham's seed a mighty nation, and that Jacob and Joseph would not be separated again before Israel passed.

The roster of Jacob's family (vv. 8-27) is given primarily as an illustration of how truly small Jacob's family was when it entered Egypt vs. when it left four centuries later (Exod. 1:5; Deut. 10:22). This list does not seem to be a comprehensive one (what of Jacob's daughters-in-law and granddaughters?). But since the number seventy represents completeness, this roster indicates that all of Jacob's family made the move. No remnant was left behind at the old homestead to keep an eye on things until the rest could return.

And who is it that went ahead of the family to arrange the reunion of Jacob and Joseph? It was Judah, the one brother most responsible for separating father and son decades earlier. When Joseph went to meet the caravan, the reunion with his father (v. 29) becomes one of the most touching scenes in Scripture.

Read Genesis 47. A confusing theme in this section is the attitude Egyptians held towards shepherds. Joseph's claim that they all were "an abomination to the Egyptians" (46:34) has puzzled scholars because there exists nothing in Egyptian literature that expresses such disdain, and Pharaoh later entrusted his flocks to the care of Joseph's brothers (v. 6). What unpleasantness, then, could Joseph have been attempting to avoid when he "coached" his brothers for their audience with Pharaoh? Perhaps Joseph meant that Egyptians despised *foreign* shepherds. It is known that, during this period, strained relations existed between Egyptians and an ethnic group known as the Hyksos who were from the same region as Jacob's family. The Egyptians derogatorily referred to them as "shepherd kings."

Another possibility is that Joseph meant wealthy Egyptians found shepherding an "abomination," i.e. they thought it was beneath them. By being honest about their occupation, Pharaoh would be assured that he wasn't welcoming a family who would mooch off the government in the middle of a famine. Rather, Joseph hoped his family would receive a favorable welcome in Egypt, be allowed to live separately on their own, and even enjoy a decent living as stewards of Pharaoh's flocks and herds.

When Jacob was introduced, he blessed Pharaoh, and rightfully so since the regent had done so much to bless the family of Israel. As the family settled in Goshen (known to the narrator as "the land of Rameses," Exod. 12:37), Joseph kept his promise and provided for all his family. The famine, however, worsened in Egypt. The remainder of Gen. 47 provides further details of Joseph's actions to save Egypt and enrich Pharaoh. The people first exchanged their money, then their livestock, and finally their own land for food. This practice led to all of Egypt's land and wealth being centrally owned by the government, and it contributed to Egypt's rise to dominance in the ancient world.

A fifth of the harvest that the people paid as rent was a much lower percentage than exemplified elsewhere in the ancient Near East (a third was more common). Joseph's shrewd management skills brought blessings to Pharaoh and the entire nation of Egypt, a fulfillment of God's promise to Abraham (12:3). It's also worth pointing out that Joseph did nothing to enrich himself during this period. He was unselfishly faithful to Pharaoh in all things, and the people considered him to be a kind, not cruel, administrator.

While the Egyptians suffered through the famine, Jacob's family prospered and "multiplied greatly." Within 400 years, they would go from a small group of 70 to numbering 603,550 fighting men on the occasion of the Exodus (Num. 1:45-46). As for Jacob, he knew his days were drawing to a close, so he made Joseph swear to him that he would be buried in Canaan. Even in his death, the patriarch wanted to declare his great faith in the promises of God.

APPLICATION

Baby Boomers. One of the most important details in this section is how the family of Israel grew significantly in population while Egypt suffered or was barely getting by. Indeed, the massive population explosion was exactly what the Pharaoh of Exodus was attempting to curb (1:9-22). Such is a reminder that blessing, fertility, and life remain the sole prerogatives of the Lord. Just when we think that death and destruction are our fate or lot, he surprises us with life and resurrection. What God did for Israel in Egyptian bondage, he can do for spiritual Israel whenever and wherever she faces persecution and suffering. The church of Christ is never in real danger of extinction as long as we serve a Commander-in-Chief who has never known defeat.

The Shrewd Manager. Though Joseph primarily serves as an incredible example of grace and forgiveness toward his brothers, he also shines as a model employee. The conclusion of Gen. 47 notes how Joseph shrewdly orchestrated a purchasing program to supply Egyptians with food, and at a cost, but a cost well below the cultural norm. To give the food away for free would have been ill-advised. Selling it for a fifth instead of a third (the norm) displayed Joseph's magnanimity. But it is the last detail, that he did not attempt to enrich himself at the people's expense, that is the most important. As Pharaoh's servant, Joseph sought to serve Pharaoh before himself. In the New Testament, Christians are called to serve their employer sincerely as if serving the Lord Jesus Christ (Col. 3:22-24).

Extended Stay. It seems that Jacob and his family went down to Egypt somewhat expecting to return home to Canaan after the famine had abated. But seventeen years later, even after their father had died, they remained. In fact, Jacob's family sojourned in Egypt for more than four centuries until God brought them out in a mighty way just as he had prophesied to Abraham (15:13-14). Funny, isn't it, how our plans for the future so rarely turn out as we expected or intended? Perhaps our focus should not be on the length of our stay in any one place, but rather on how we conduct ourselves while we are there. We have no control over the morrow, only our motives and actions. Let us resolve to control only what is in our power and allow God to handle the rest.

CONCLUSION

As he had declared to Pharaoh, Jacob had lived a difficult life and his sojourn on earth was about to end. But God had been faithful to the patriarch, particularly through the providential guidance and care that had been exercised concerning Joseph, and thereby to Jacob's entire family. The family of Jacob had been reunited with Joseph and spared the worst of the famine. For all of his spiritually-troubled past, Jacob died full of faith, but not before receiving from God a powerful glimpse into the future.

QUESTIONS FOR REFLECTION

1. Why did Jacob appear to be apprehensive about leaving Canaan? What assurances did God give him?

2. What was the geographical importance of Beersheba?

3. Why did Joseph coach his brothers to list "shepherd" as their occupation?

4. Where did Jacob and his family settle in Egypt?

5. Through shrewd management, how did Joseph legally transfer ownership of much of Egypt to Pharaoh?

QUESTIONS FOR DISCUSSION

1. In what ways did Jacob's family flourish in Egypt? In what ways do God's people today still thrive despite suffering and sojourning in a land not their own?

2. What traits of an honorable, godly employee can we see in Joseph in his life's story? How is Joseph's example different from many other government officials?

3. When they made the move to Egypt, Jacob's family likely did not believe it would be four centuries before they returned to Canaan. How can our faith in God be undermined when our expectations for the future are not realized?

4. Why is it important to accurately discern the things that are and are not in our control? In what ways have you attempted to control things that were really beyond your control? What was the result of those occasions?

12

JACOB'S BLESSING

GENESIS 48-49

Objective: To study Jacob's final blessing on his sons
and its importance to the future of Israel's tribes

INTRODUCTION

After seventeen years in Egypt, Jacob knew the end of his life was immi-
nent, and it was now time to impart a final blessing to his sons. The patriarchal blessing was a means of symbolically passing on the promises of God
to the next generation. We have seen multiple occasions where a father's
blessing to his son held significant sway over future events; Jacob's blessing
of his sons is a sort of capstone to this idea in Genesis.

What follows is unprecedented in Scripture. So far, no word of prophecy has come from mortal lips, and no recorded words have been uttered
on one's deathbed. But Jacob was given a glimpse of the future, to the time
when the Promised Land would be conquered and settled, and even beyond. As he blessed his sons, the events of the future unfolded before his
dim eyes like movie scenes.

EXAMINATION

Read Genesis 48. Notified that his father was ill, Joseph brought his two sons (now aged about twenty years) to see their grandfather. Jacob had to summon his strength in order to sit up in bed, but even at such an advanced age, Jacob still remembered and rehearsed the great promise that God had made to him at Bethel, notably the promise to make the patriarch "fruitful and multiply" him (v. 4).

Joseph presented Manasseh (the oldest) at Jacob's right hand and Ephraim (the youngest) at his father's left so that Manasseh would receive the firstborn blessing. The right hand was considered the position of privilege, strength, and honor. But in a twist that should by now come as no real surprise in our study of Genesis, Jacob expressed his preference for the younger and gave Ephraim the birthright. To Joseph specifically, Jacob gave the property he had obtained at Shechem (33:19). His reference to it as land "that I took from the hand of the Amorites with my sword and with my bow" (v. 22) points to an event not preserved in Genesis.

In many ways, Joseph's two sons indeed took his place among the tribes of Israel. Here, Jacob predicted that Ephraim would become greater than his older brother. In the first census taken after the Exodus, the tribe of Ephraim numbered 40,500 to Manasseh's 32,200 (Num. 1:33, 35). It is a very significant fact that, in the second census, the combined tribes of Ephraim and Manasseh outnumbered those of Reuben and Simeon. In the Judges period, Ephraim became quite powerful; during the divided monarchy, the tribe became synonymous for the entire northern kingdom of Israel (e.g. Isa. 7:9; Hos. 5:3; 7:1).

Read Genesis 49. Jacob acknowledged Reuben as the true firstborn, but then rebuked him for his character. Reuben lost the double inheritance due him because he had committed adultery with his father's concubine (35:22). Consequently, Jacob called him "unstable as water" (v. 4), which means Jacob considered Reuben's act to have been irresponsible, impetuous, and immoral. A single moment of indiscretion, whether motivated by ambition or passion, had cost Reuben the blessing of the firstborn.

The prophecy that Reuben's tribe would "not have preeminence" indeed came true. In the wilderness, two of the leaders in Korah's rebellion were Reubenites (cf. Num. 16; 26:5-10); it is thought that this rebellion was an attempt to reassert Reuben's influence in Israel. By the time of David, the tribe of Reuben is no longer mentioned and likely had merged with the tribe of Gad at this point.

Given Reuben's demotion, Simeon and Levi were next in line to receive the firstborn birthright. But they too were dismissed as a result of their "violence" at Shechem (34:25). Jacob consequently distanced himself from Simeon and Levi as he had from Reuben.

As it turned out, the tribes of Simeon and Levi were indeed scattered throughout the land of Israel, but in different ways and for very different reasons. At the first census, the Simeonites numbered 59,300, but sank to only 22,000 a generation later (Num. 1:23; 26:14; cf. 25:1-14). When it came time to portion out the land of Canaan, Simeon was given a small allotment within Judah's territory (Josh. 19:1, 9). From that point on, the tribe's role in Israel's history was largely insignificant.

The tribe of Levi, on the other hand, redeemed itself. At Sinai, they sided with Moses in the golden calf episode and were in turn given the honor of the priesthood (Exod. 32:28-29). The tribe did not receive a territorial allotment in Canaan (Num. 18:20; Deut. 10:9), but they were apportioned 48 cities throughout Israel (Num. 35:7).

The lengthiest part of Jacob's last will and testament applies to Judah, the one who would eventually assume rule over all Israel. Originating here is the popular phrase "lion of Judah." Jacob envisioned for Judah both dominion and abundance. That Judah dominated the rest of Israel almost goes without saying. The tribe was the largest in both censuses in the wilderness (Num. 1:27; 26:22), and they held the privileged position of being camped just to the east of the Tabernacle (Num. 2:3). Beginning with David's ascendancy, one of his sons sat on the throne until the Babylonian Exile (cf. 2 Sam. 7:16). Another of David's descendants, Zerubbabel, led the Jews out of exile and served as their first governor (cf. Ezra 2:2).

The blessing on the tribe of Zebulun is rather odd; their land-allotment in Canaan never bordered Galilee or the Mediterranean (cf. Josh. 19:10-16). So why did Zebulun receive a maritime blessing? Though Zebulun never geographically touched the sea, the Philistines and Phoenicians employed several men from the tribe in sea trade. The tribe certainly lived near enough to the coast to profit from maritime activity. Further mention of Zebulun in the Old Testament is positive. They readily answered Barak's call to oppose the Canaanite threat (Judg. 4:10; 5:14, 18), as well as Gideon's summons to ambush the Midianites (Judg. 6:35). They supplied David with 50,000 experienced, well-equipped, and deeply loyal troops (1 Chron. 12:33).

Issachar is said to be "a strong donkey" (v. 14) at rest between… And this is where it becomes confusing. English translations render the Hebrew *mishpetayim* variously as "sheepfolds" (ESV) and "saddlebags" (HCSB). Which is it? In the word's only other occurrence (Judg 5:16), the meaning is almost certainly "sheepfolds." But it's also possible for the word to mean saddlebags, and that translation seems best here given the context. The Carmel and Gilboa mountain ranges did surround Issachar's land-allotment in Canaan like two saddlebags. Not much else is mentioned about the tribe of Issachar in the rest of Scripture, though they did contribute a judge (Tola, Judg. 10:1) and two kings (Baasha and Elah, 1 Kgs. 15:27; 16:8). In David's day, the tribe was known for her "men who understood the times and knew what Israel should do" (1 Chron. 12:32).

In the wilderness, the tribe of Dan was quite large, second only to Judah (Num. 2:26; 26:43), and in Jacob's blessing, it enjoyed the favored place of seventh in line. But the tribe eventually dwindled in size. Only one son is attributed to Dan (46:23), and in his genealogies, the Chronicler gives the tribe no mention whatsoever. Whenever Israel traveled towards Canaan, Dan was at the end of the line (Num. 10:25). What is more startling is Dan's absence from Revelation's list of the tribes of Israel (Rev. 7:5–8).

According to Jacob's imagery in v. 17, Dan would be like a small snake biting a large horse. The tribe's most glorious moment was Samson's career as a judge, his guerrilla tactics decimating the more powerful Philistines. But with these menacing neighbors on their southern border, the tribe failed to conquer their territory (Judg. 1:34-35), and they eventually relocated to the northern region of Canaan (Josh. 19:47; Judg. 18). It is therefore no wonder that Jacob's blessing of Dan is punctuated with an appeal to God's deliverance (v. 18), an appeal that only a father could make on behalf of his son. With so many threats lying before Dan (and for that matter, all of Jacob's sons), how could he possibly survive without divine intervention?

The future allotment of Gad lay east of the Jordan, and the tribe was often raided by its neighbors, including the Ammonites, Moabites, Arameans, and Assyrians. But Gad's military was a formidable threat (1 Chron. 5:18; 12:8; cf. Deut. 33:20). Jacob's blessing, then, warns that the tribe would have more than its fair share of skirmishes, but it would also experience more than its fair share of victories, though (like Dan) such victories would come using guerrilla tactics.

Asher's descendants settled in a very fertile area west of Galilee and north of Mount Carmel (Josh 19:24-31), running all the way to Phoenicia, one that proved quite prosperous for the tribe (Deut. 33:24). Their provision of "royal delicacies" is supposed by most scholars to indicate the tribe furnished food for early Canaanite rulers until these pagan kings were vanquished by Barak and Deborah.

Jacob's blessing of Naphtali has proven impossible to interpret. One alternative pictures Naphtali as a free-roaming deer that eventually settles down to birth fawns in a fold, or as a great tree that puts down deep roots and prospers. Those who interpret Jacob's words negatively point to when Naphtali would consent to co-existence with the Canaanites instead of expelling them (Judg. 1:33). They were subsequently oppressed by the Canaanites until the tribe, led by native son Barak and prophetess Deborah, won a decisive victory.

Judah was arguably promised the greatest of riches, but when he blessed Joseph, Jacob's affection for his favored son became very evident. The patriarch anticipated for his favorite son divine deliverance from all of Joseph's enemies. His brothers had tried "bitterly" to do away with Joseph, but Jacob knew they had not been successful due to God's power and provision. Jacob boasts that this blessing on Joseph would be greater than the one given to Abraham and Isaac, and that nothing in heaven or below the earth could negate it as long as God showed Joseph such favor.

Jacob cryptically called Benjamin "a ravenous wolf," a metaphor that is typically interpreted as predatory, and that description is spot-on. It was a Benjamite, Ehud, who assassinated Eglon (Judg. 3:15-30), and the tribe also joined Deborah and Barak against the Canaanites (Judg. 5:14). Later in the Judges period, their army of 26,700 massacred 40,000 enemy troops in two days of bloody civil war (20:14-25). Men of Benjamin were known to be "mighty warriors" with bows and slingshots (1 Chron. 8:40; 12:2).

APPLICATION

Faith in Death. Jacob's great faith on his deathbed is absolutely remarkable for several reasons. When Jacob spoke of Abraham's and Isaac's relationship with God (48:15), he used Hebrew verb forms that insinuated completed action (which makes sense as both were no longer living). But when he spoke of God's action, he used participles that translate to continuous or on-going action. Abraham was dead; so was Isaac, and Jacob would soon join them. But the patriarch made clear to his family that God wasn't going anywhere. Jacob had no reason to fear, and neither did his tribe. He also promised that God would restore Israel, not to "Canaan," but "to the land of your fathers." "Canaan" was a geo-political term; by calling it "the land of your fathers," Jacob affirmed that it rightfully belonged to Abraham's descendants. God had sworn to it, and he would be faithful, for none of his promises can ever fail. When we meet our own deaths, may we do so confident that God will continue to bless those we leave behind, and may we anticipate the future consummation of all his promises in Christ.

Judah's Final Vindication. Judah's dominance and the establishment of David's throne "forever" found their ultimate fulfillment in Christ (Heb. 1:8), the son of Judah (Matt. 1:2), who anticipated the reception of a glorious throne in the world to come (Matt. 19:28). Even now, though he is the ascended Lord exalted to God's right hand, we anticipate with longing the day when the King of kings "will tread the winepress of the fury of the wrath of God the Almighty" (Rev. 19:15), cause every knee to bow to him (Phil. 2:10), and receive "the obedience of the peoples" (Gen. 49:10). With a roar, the Lion of Judah "shall speak peace to the nations; his rule shall be … to the ends of the earth" (Zech. 9:10), "and he shall reign forever and ever" (Rev. 11:15). For all his struggles of faith, Judah's final vindication was that God brought forth the Savior of the world through his seed. We need not be perfect—just faithful—to be a wondrous part of God's grand scheme to unite everything in heaven and earth under the reign of his Son.

Cut Off. To be perfectly candid, Dan married himself out of the covenant promises. One has to wonder if the decline of the tribe of Dan was due to its tendency to intermarry among the neighboring nations (Lev. 24:10-11; Judg. 14:1-2), which was clearly prohibited (Deut. 7:3). As mentioned previously, it is striking that Dan's name is omitted from the tribal list in Revelation. This is not just a warning against marrying someone of a different faith, or a reminder to choose your friends carefully. Rather, it is a broader cautionary tale against expecting to retain God's blessings while ignoring his will. God will keep his promises to us; he will remain faithful to us, and no one can pluck us from his hand. But we can nonetheless forfeit the blessing of our Father's house when we walk not in our Father's footsteps. Let us strive not to be like Dan and forfeit our covenant blessings because of our disobedience.

CONCLUSION

The author of Hebrews considers Jacob's blessing of his sons to be his greatest act of faith (11:21). In the face of death, it indeed requires tremendous faith in God to look forward into the future, but Jacob was confident that his death did not also mean death for the promises of God. Those would continue for the next generation. Like all the heroes of faith, Jacob recognized that his was a small part of a grander story, a temporary task in the context of a grander scheme (Heb. 11:13-16). And his children needed to know that their father's death did not also spell the death of their future—far from it.

For the people of God, death is always a new beginning.

QUESTIONS FOR REFLECTION

1. How did Genesis' preference for the younger over the older continue with Joseph's sons? What irony do you see in Joseph's objection?

2. In the time of Moses, how did the tribe of Levi go on to redeem itself from Jacob's less-than-positive blessing?

3. Besides Reuben, what tribe seems to have lost its status in Israel by the time of the New Testament?

4. Which son was predicted to enjoy regal dominance over his brothers? From which son of Jacob would the future Christ come?

5. How is the tribe of Benjamin portrayed in Jacob's blessing and their latter history?

QUESTIONS FOR DISCUSSION

6. How can we demonstrate faith in God's providence and anticipation of his promises in the face of death?

7. Why do you think tribes like Levi and Judah were able to overcome dark family histories, while Reuben and Dan were not? What made the difference?

8. Like the tribes of Levi and Judah, have you known people who overcame their family's past to go on to achieve great things? In your opinion, how did they successfully "rise above their DNA"?

9. Like the tribe of Dan, have you ever lost one of God's blessings because you ignored or disregarded his will? What happened in the aftermath? How did you feel?

10. On one hand, God was sovereign over the destinies of Jacob's sons since he knew their futures so intimately. On the other hand, God's foreknowledge did not preclude tribes like Levi from reversing Jacob's prophecy. How do we harmonize this tension: foreknowledge vs. free will?

11. Discuss this statement: "Die in the Lord for your family's sake."

13

DEATH OF JACOB & JOSEPH

GENESIS 50

Objective: To close out the Genesis story
and celebrate God's providence

INTRODUCTION

The family of Israel had now been in Egypt for many years, and their patri-arch had died. How would Abraham's offspring survive in a foreign land? This question lingers in the back of the reader's mind. In the forefront of our minds is whether Joseph and his brothers will continue to get along with one another after their father's death. The narrator answers both our inquiries by pointing to the undying love and magnificent providence of the God of Abraham.

EXAMINATION

Read Genesis 50. His sons now blessed, Jacob made them swear they would bury him in the cave of Machpelah, the family cemetery. This dying wish reflects a major theme in Genesis—the Promised Land of Canaan be-longs to Abraham's descendants. Anywhere else, including Egypt, is only a temporary stop. It had been a tremendous act of faith when Abraham had purchased a small plot of land in order to bury Sarah; Jacob maintained that faith with his dying request.

It is touching that, for his eternal resting place, Jacob specifically asked to be beside Leah (49:31), the wife he had loved less, and not Rachel. Had Jacob grown more affectionate for Laban's oldest daughter over the passing years? Was theirs always a loveless marriage?

This scene marks a remarkable consummation to Jacob's life. For much of his early existence, Jacob had resorted too often to his own sufficiency and too little to God's providence. To scorn God's gracious providence is to scorn his great promises. But on his deathbed, Jacob declared his confidence in those promises. And because the God of his fathers had been faithful to him in death (46:4), Jacob responded in kind. The patriarch's redemption was complete.

For those that could afford it, mummification was a common practice in Egypt that held great religious significance. Temple priests would remove the body's internal organs and soak the body in embalming fluid for forty days; the organs themselves were sealed in containers and buried with the body. Concerning the afterlife, Egyptian theology maintained that the corpse was the repository of the soul. Jacob's body was mummified per the custom of Egypt, but note that it was Joseph's personal physicians, not the priests, that performed the procedure, meaning the act held no religious significance to Jacob's family. That the Egyptians mourned Jacob's passing for 70 days is significant; according to the Greek historian Diodorus, 72 days was the customary period of mourning for Pharaoh.

After receiving permission from Pharaoh to bury Jacob in Canaan, Joseph led the funeral procession to the cave of Machpelah. As is still the case today, the amount of pomp and circumstance over a person's passing signified their importance (cf. 2 Chron. 21:20), so the sight of so many Egyptian dignitaries and officials making this journey to pay their final respects had to have been an impressive one. It is remarkable to think that Abraham had been a wealthy, but comparatively unremarkable, nomad from Ur. The death of his grandson, however, was memorialized by a veritable Who's Who of Egypt. God was fulfilling his promise to Abraham: "I will bless you and make your name great" (12:2).

Bruce Waltke's summary of Jacob's legacy bears repeating in full:

This scene concludes Jacob's finest hour. On his death-bed—a scene extending from 47:28 to 49:32—Jacob has assumed total and dynamic leadership of the family. Even Joseph bows down to him. Jacob gives the double blessing to the deserving firstborn son of the wife he loves, not to the detestable firstborn of Leah. With prophetic insight, he crosses his hands against even Joseph the traditionalist. Without wavering, he looks forward to Israel's divine destiny in the land of promise. Renouncing even his love for Rachel, his last words instruct his sons to bury him with his unloved wife so he can rest in faith with his fathers.

At the beginning of the act he comes trepidly to Egypt, not for its riches, comforts, and security, but out of love for a son. While showing great respect and sensitivity to Pharaoh, he never bows his knee to the Egyptian but instead, as the greater, blesses the lesser. Isaac's old age shamed his youth, but Jacob's redeems his, just as Judah's heroic self-sacrifice redeems his tragic beginnings.

All honor Jacob in his death. Joseph and his brothers mourn their father's death and faithfully carry out his instructions to bury him in the ancestral grave. The Egyptians mourn him for two and half months as they would mourn their king. The skilled physicians embalm him for forty days, and the most senior dignitaries both from Pharaoh's own court and from the whole empire bear Jacob's body homeward from Egypt to Canaan in a grand and grave funeral cortege. With these details the narrator asserts Jacob's true redemption and exaltation.

Returning to Egypt, Joseph's brothers worried his forgiving spirit had been a ruse all along, and they sought his forgiveness for the first time. They acknowledged their betrayal as "sin," "evil," and a "transgression." The brothers likely put words in daddy's mouth in a self-serving manner (v. 17), and sadly, that can happen in families when a loved one passes: "Daddy wouldn't have wanted you to…" or "Your mother would have wanted you to…" But the brothers were carrying a lot of guilt because sin haunts the offender for a very long time—forgiving self is often the most difficult forgiveness to grant. Note that they dared not identify themselves to Joseph as his "brothers," but as "servants of the God of your father."

Joseph's response in vv. 19-20 stands, not only as the perfect summary of Genesis, but also as a shadow of how the rest of human history would unfold with God at the helm. At the beginning of Genesis, Adam and Eve attempted to erase the line distinguishing God from man (3:5-6); here, Joseph refused to cross that line, acknowledging that some things belong to God alone (cf. Rom. 12:19). Joseph understood that life is not a series of unfortunate events, but rather events that unfold under the sovereign watch of God. At times, it requires tremendous faith to believe this truth, but God will never allow an event to occur that he cannot use to glorify himself and redeem our brokenness.

Exhibiting remarkable perspective, Joseph assured his brothers that he would use his position of influence to care for them and their families. Such a response on Joseph's part can only be borne within the heart of one absolutely confident that God is in control, that God is crafting a wondrous story of redemption and grace.

Joseph himself was able to see the births of his great-grandchildren, which in the ancient Near East was considered proof of immense divine blessing or, secularly, great fortune. Joseph lived to the age of 110, considered by ancient Egyptians to be an ideal age, though most Egyptians did not live past forty or fifty.

APPLICATION

Death Has No Power. In Christ, death has no victory. But it is indeed a cruel master, and the Old Testament portrays it in not so flattering terms. It is depicted as a fleeing shadow (Job 14:2), the journey of no return (Job 16:22), the king of terrors (Job 18:14), and a return to the dust (Psa. 104:29). The Bible's most iconic and memorable image is John's depiction of death as a rider astride a pale horse (Rev. 6:8). But even though the passing of a loved one causes immense grief as it did for Jacob's family, Christians have been promised that death is not the end. In light of the Resurrection, "Death is swallowed up in victory" (1 Cor 15:54). There is no reason, therefore, why our family and friends should have to grieve so painfully when we pass from this life. As Jacob and Joseph exhorted Israel to trust in God, encourage your family to do the same. Live a life of faith so that they are not forced to grieve as those who have no hope (1 Thess. 4:13). Die in Christ for their sake and your own; for in Christ, death has no victory.

The Power of Guilt. Guilt can be as powerful a force as death. More than seventeen years after coming to Egypt, Joseph's brothers still were haunted by their selling him into slavery. They were painfully aware of the suffering they had caused. Even in Gen. 50, they could not bring themselves to be completely honest, preferring instead to hide behind the sacred cow of their dead father's moral authority. God does not want us to feel any more guilt than is necessary to drive us into his arms (2 Cor. 7:10). God is not in the guilt-business because guilt imprisons; his grace liberates (John 8:36). And the only way that grace can free us from the prison of guilt is for us to own up to our sins. Joseph's brothers finally did that in Gen. 50, and as far as we can tell, healing finally took place in their hearts. Perhaps one of the promises of God you have yet to put your faith in is the one of 1 John 1:9. "If we confess our sins, he is faithful and just to forgive us our sins and to cleanse us from all unrighteousness." If God has forgiven us, how are we not also obligated to do the same?

CONCLUSION

Along with Joseph's bones, Israel would linger in Egypt for a few centuries. A Pharaoh would arise that did not know Joseph, and Israel suffered. But the same God who had remembered Noah and provided for Abraham would visit his people in their suffering. The story of God and his love would continue with Moses and the Exodus. Indeed, the rest of Scripture echoes with the message of Genesis: God is always faithful to his people.

QUESTIONS FOR REFLECTION

1. How/why was Jacob's burial request a statement of faith?

2. Who mummified Jacob? Why was this significant?

3. How long was Jacob mourned by the Egyptians?

4. Fill in the blank: "Life is not a series of _____ events, but rather events that unfold under the _____ watch of ___."

5. How old was Joseph when he died? Why was this significant for Egyptians?

QUESTIONS FOR DISCUSSION

1. Why can Christians still be positive and hopeful when a loved one dies?

2. How many different ways does the Bible speak of death? In your opinion, which is the most sinister or troubling?

3. Explain this statement: "God does not want us to feel any more guilt than is necessary to drive us into his arms."

4. How have you seen guilt carried around as an unnecessary weight?

5. In what ways has this study of Genesis helped you trust more in God and his providence?

6. What lesson in this study of Genesis has been the most meaningful to you?

Made in the USA
Columbia, SC
22 March 2024

33232312R00055